"At the Instance of Benjamin Franklin"

A Brief History of the
Library Company of Philadelphia

Francesco Lazzarini, *Benjamin Franklin*. Marble sculpture, ca. 1792, commissioned by William Bingham for the Library Company's first building.

"At the Instance of Benjamin Franklin"

A Brief History of the Library Company of Philadelphia

REVISED AND ENLARGED EDITION

PRINTED FOR THE LIBRARY COMPANY OF PHILADELPHIA

by YORK GRAPHIC SERVICES, INC.

1995

©1995 by the Library Company of Philadelphia,
1314 Locust Street, Philadelphia, PA 19107

Printed in the United States of America
by York Graphic Services, Inc.

ISBN 0-914076-90-6

Cover illustration: Detail of *Library and Surgeon's Hall, Fifth-street,*
one of the engravings in William Birch's *The City of Philadelphia*
(Philadelphia, 1800). The entire plate is reproduced on page 29
of this book.

The type ornaments on the title page are reproduced from the
title page of Benjamin Franklin's 1734 printing of
The Constitutions of the Free-Masons.

Photography by Will Brown.

On July 1, 1731, Benjamin Franklin and a number of his fellow members of the Junto drew up "Articles of Agreement" to found a library. The Junto was a discussion group of young men seeking social, economic, intellectual, and political advancement. When they foundered on a point of fact or had a difference of opinion, they needed a printed authority to settle the matter. In colonial Pennsylvania at the time there were not many books. Standard English reference works were expensive and difficult to obtain. Franklin and his friends were mostly mechanics of moderate means. None alone could have afforded a representative library nor, indeed, many imported books. By pooling their resources in pragmatic Franklinian fashion, they could. The contribution of each created the book capital of all.

Fifty subscribers invested forty shillings each and promised to pay ten shillings a year thereafter to buy books and maintain a shareholder's library. Thus "the Mother of all American Subscription Libraries" was established. A seal was decided upon with the device "Two Books open, Each encompass'd with Glory, or Beams of Light, between which water streaming from above into an Urn below, thence issues at many Vents into lesser Urns, and Motto, circumscribing the whole, *Communiter Bona profundere Deum est.*" This translates freely as "To pour forth benefits for the common good is divine." The silversmith Philip Syng engraved the seal. The first list of desiderata to stock the shelves was sent to London on March 31, 1732, and by autumn that order, less a few books found to be unobtainable, arrived. James Logan, "the best Judge of Books in these parts," had assisted in the choice, and it was a representative one.

Were one to draw up a list of the works most commonly found in colonial American libraries, and probably provincial English libraries, the early selection of the Library Company could serve as a pattern. In the earlier ecclesiastical and collegiate libraries of British America the choice of books was superimposed from without for theological or educational purposes and reflected the formal learning of donor or teacher. In the Library Company the desire for the book stemmed from the prospective reader.

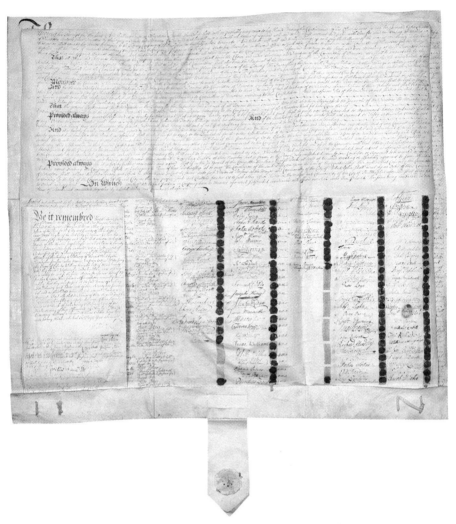

Articles of Association. Manuscript on vellum, Philadelphia, July 1, 1731.

Gifts in kind and in cash began to increase the library's book and financial resources, as indeed they have continued to do to this day. In February 1733, Librarian Louis Timothée, Secretary Joseph Breintnall, and Franklin presented a number of volumes, including *A Collection of Several Pieces*, by John Locke; *Logic: or, the Art of Thinking*, by the Port Royalists Arnauld and Nicole, which Franklin in his autobiography said he had read at the age of sixteen; Plutarch's *Morals* in the translation of Philemon Holland; Lewis Roberts's

Merchants Mappe of Commerce; and others. A bit later, William Rawle added a set of Spenser's *Works* to the collection, and Francis Richardson gave several volumes, among them Francis Bacon's *Sylva Sylvarum*. That same year the Proprietor Thomas Penn sent a print of an orrery to the infant institution, "where it was fram'd & hung up at our late annual Election of Officers, when the Presenter was frequently named with just Gratitude." Much more Penn bounty was hoped for.

In the spring of 1735 a florid address was delivered to John Penn, then in residence at Pennsbury, that concluded: "That Virtue, Learning & true Religion may increase and flourish, under the Encouragement and Protection of your honourable House, is our earnest and hearty Endeavour." Penn acknowledged the Library Company's thinly veiled request for patronage with thanks. More generous was the unsolicited gift of £34 sterling that arrived in the summer of 1738 from Walter Sydserfe, a Scottish-born physician and planter of Antigua, who had heard of the establishment of the library from John Sober, one of its original directors. A good start had been made.

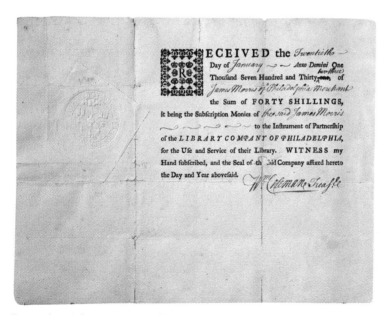

Receipt for a Library Company Share, January 20, 1733. Printed by Franklin.

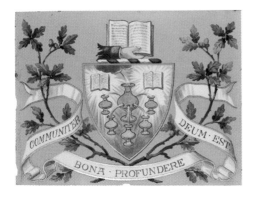

Minton, Hollis & Co., *Fireplace tile*, 1882. From the Librarian's office in the Ridgway Building, depicting coat of arms.

Joseph Breintnall, *Letter to Thomas Hopkinson*. Philadelphia, March 31, 1732. The first order of books.

Tin Suggestion Box,
ca. 1750.

By the time the library issued its earliest surviving printed catalogue in 1741, the general mix of its collection for over a century was established. Excluding gifts, historical works, broadly defined, accounted for approximately one-third of the total holdings. These included geographical books and accounts of voyages and travels, which latter category the Library Company emphasized until comparatively recently. Literature—plays and poems mostly—comprised a little more than twenty percent, approximately the same proportion as science. Theology accounted for only one tenth of the titles. This was in

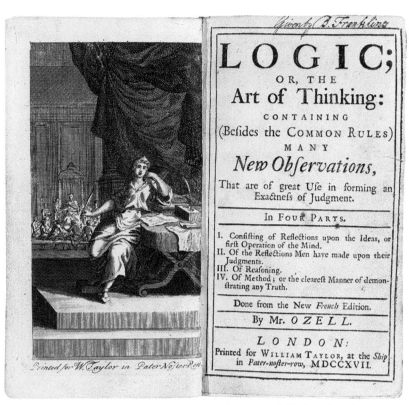

[Antoine Arnaud and Pierre Nicole], *Logic; Or, the Art of Thinking*. London, 1717. Benjamin Franklin's copy, given to the Library Company in 1733. In his *Autobiography* Franklin said that this book helped him form "an Exactness of Judgment."

marked contrast to the earlier libraries of Harvard and Yale but a harbinger of other popular libraries that were founded later. Such a diminution of printed religiosity was a characteristic difference between the theological seventeenth century in the British colonies and the deistical eighteenth century. To conclude the selection, it should be noted that philosophy matched theology in numbers and that economics and such social sciences, the arts, linguistics, and the indefinables accounted for the rest. Bought for many years through the agency of the Quaker merchant and naturalist of London, Peter Collinson, this remained the basic weighting of book selection until the decline of the proprietary libraries in the last half of the nineteenth century.

The Library Company flourished because it adopted a purchasing policy that was responsive to the needs of its intellectually alert, eco-

A *Catalogue of Books Belonging to the Library Company of Philadelphia.* Philadelphia: Printed by B. Franklin, 1741. The earliest extant catalogue of the Library Company; Franklin also printed broadside catalogues in 1733 and 1735, of which no copies have survived.

nomically ambitious, but non-elite membership. Its successful example was quickly copied along the Atlantic seaboard from Salem to Charleston. It was Franklin's opinion that "these Libraries have improved the general Conversation of Americans, made the common Tradesmen and Farmers as intelligent as most Gentlemen from other Countries, and perhaps have contributed in some Degree to the Stand so generally made throughout the Colonies in Defence of their Priviledges."

The Library soon became not only an increasing collection of books but also a full-fledged cabinet of curiosities in the Renaissance mode. Donors deposited in its rooms antique coins, fossils, fauna preserved in spirits, unusual geological specimens, tanned skins, and other oddities. In accordance with its role as an all-embracing cultural institution, the Library Company also participated in the increasingly popular scientific experimentation of its day.

At first housed in a room in the librarian's lodgings, the burgeoning accumulation became too much for private quarters. When John Penn sent an air pump to the quasi-learned society, the directors had to take a major step to house it properly. The instrument arrived early in 1739. A handsome cabinet was commissioned for it. That glass-fronted case survives as the earliest extant example of American-made

THE GIFT OF THE HONOURABLE
JOHN PENN, Efq. MDCCXXXVIII.

John Harrison, *Air-Pump Case*. [Philadelphia, 1739]. Built to house a gift of scientific glassware from John Penn, which Franklin used in his electrical experiments. It is the earliest surviving piece of architectural furniture in the Palladian style made in America.

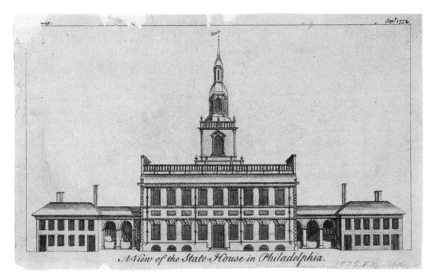

George Heap, A *View of the State House in Philadelphia*. Engraving from *The Gentleman's Magazine*, London, 1752.

Palladian architectural furniture. Arrangements were promptly made to move the books, cabinet of curiosities, and air pump case into rooms on the second floor of the newly finished west wing of the State House (now Independence Hall). It was there that Franklin and his associates performed their first experiments in electricity. Exactly when Collinson sent over to the Philadelphians a hollow glass tube that introduced them to the intriguing phenomenon of static electricity is not known. There is a record of the arrival of a "Trunk of Books, Glass Tubes &c." in the summer of 1742, but Franklin, reminiscing later, gave other dates for the beginning of the experiments. They must have been well under way by 1747, when "a compleat Electrical Apparatus" was received from Thomas Penn.

Suitably settled, the library could turn its attention to making its holdings known. Although broadsheet catalogues of the Library Company's books may have been issued in 1733 and 1735, no copy of either survives. An existing small octavo of fifty-six pages, printed by Franklin and issued in 1741, lists the 375 titles then in the library. As eighteenth-century catalogues go, it was a good one, the first American library catalogue to give titles at some length as well as place and date of publication. Franklin wrote "A Short Account of the Library" to fill a final blank page. No waste, no want. Franklin noted that the library was open Saturday afternoons from four until eight o'clock.

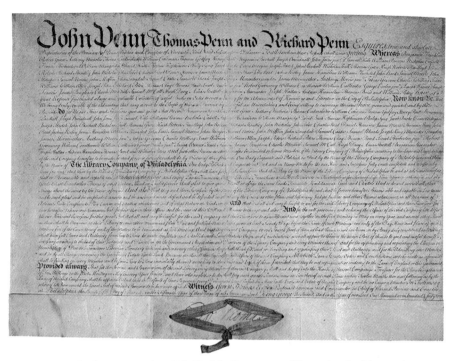

Original Charter, Signed on Behalf of the Proprietors of Pennsylvania. Manuscript on vellum, Philadelphia, March 25, 1742.

Members could borrow books freely and without charge. Nonmembers could borrow books by depositing their value as security "and paying a small Acknowledgment for the Reading." In the early days this reading fee was apparently either never collected or discontinued; it does not appear as income in the first financial reports.

With a catalogue available, the books shelved in the State House wing, regular orders of books sent to the volunteer agent Collinson, and annual shipments received from London, the Library Company again sought the patronage of the proprietors of Pennsylvania. What the directors really wanted was a handsome benefaction in books or cash. They did get a plot of land for a hoped-for building of their own and, on March 24, 1742, a charter from John, Thomas, and Richard Penn, issued in their name by Governor George Thomas. By it, since the members had "at great expense, purchased a large and valuable collection of useful books, in order to erect a library for the advancement of knowledge and literature in the city of Philadelphia," there was created "one body corporate and politic in deed." The charter was printed in 1746, together with the by-laws and a supplementary catalogue.

The first librarian, Louis Timothée, or Timothy as he became, left after a short tenure to become Franklin's printing partner in Charleston. For a very brief period, Franklin himself took on the bibliothecal responsibility. He was succeeded by the erstwhile shoemaker and self-trained surveyor William Parsons, who served from 1734 to 1746. Parsons was followed as librarian by Robert Greenway, who remained in office for seventeen years.

The more important functionary of the institution was the secretary, at first the scrivener and amateur botanist Joseph Breintnall. He kept the minutes and wrote the letters ordering books to Collinson,

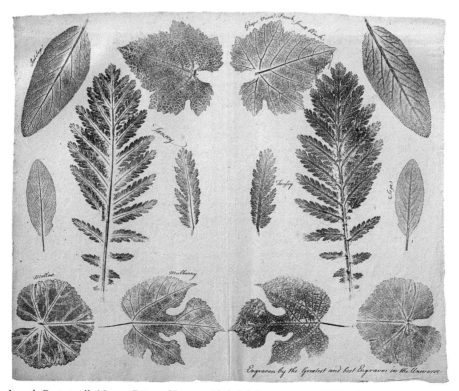

Joseph Breintnall, *Nature Prints of Leaves*. Philadelphia, 1731–44. Gift of his widow, 1746.

who faithfully carried out the Library Company's requests for over a quarter of a century. After Breintnall's death in 1746 it was Franklin who performed the secretarial duties. Despite his mythical reputation as the careful, methodical "Poor Richard," Franklin was careless about the Library Company's records. When he went to England in 1757, first the schoolmaster Francis Alison and then young Francis Hopkinson served as secretary. When Hopkinson took custody of the Library Company's box, which Franklin had left with his wife, he found that the notes of minutes taken on separate pieces of paper during the printer-politician's years in office were scattered and imperfect. To create a permanent record, Hopkinson copied into a book all the minutes of the Library Company from the beginning, although lacunae exist for some periods in the 1740s and 1750s.

The books that flowed regularly across the Atlantic from the London bookshops had the same mix of subject matter as the first shipments. There were recent works of history and travel, some poems, plays and novels, and standard vade mecums (portable reference books) and popularizations in the field of practical arts and sciences. Franklin wrote that "in the Scheme of the Library I had provided only for English Books." Likewise, in his College of Philadelphia he provided only a good English education. Although Provost William Smith stressed a classical education more than Franklin had hoped, the members of the Library Company, with little Latin and less Greek, bought very few books that were not in English.

Treasures-to-be came in 1755 and 1758 in the boxes from Collinson in the form of his own copies of a score of seventeenth-century accounts of the newly established British colonies in America. Among them were such classics of colonization as Strachey's *Lawes*, Mourt's *Relation*, and John Smith's *Generall Historie of Virginia*. New catalogues were issued in 1757 and 1764.

At the same time the museum aspect of the Library Company and its role as a scientific institution were not neglected. In 1752 a surprise gift of a collection of Roman coins came from Charles Gray, a Tory member of Parliament from Colchester, who later voted against the repeal of the Stamp Act. Two years later Charles Swaine deposited in the Library Company's room some tools and Eskimo parkas that were the only tangible fruits of the abortive Philadelphia-financed expedition to seek a Northwest Passage. In the care of Francis

John Smith, *The Generall Historie of Virginia, New-England and the Summer Isles.*
London, 1624. Gift of the naturalist Peter Collinson, with his manuscript notes.

American Weekly Mercury.
Philadelphia: Printed by
Andrew Bradford,
December 22, 1719. Joseph
Breintnall's copy, and the only
known copy of the first issue.

Mummy's Hand. Gift of the artist Benjamin West, 1767.

Hopkinson, Benjamin West sent over the hand of a mummified Egyptian princess. The institution's microscope and telescope were frequently requested for use by various scientific investigators. The latter at one time had to be sent to the London instrument maker James Short to be repaired, and in 1769 it was used by Owen Biddle to observe the transit of Venus from Cape Henlopen.

Among those who guided the Library Company's destiny in the years before the Revolution were the silversmith Philip Syng, Dr. Thomas Cadwalader, the schoolmaster Francis Alison, the builder-architect Samuel Rhoads, secretary Richard Peters of the Governor's Council, and a bit later the merchant-patriot Charles Thomson and John Dickinson, the "Pennsylvania Farmer."

The library kept growing, in part by absorbing some of its own progeny. The Union Library, founded in 1746, into which had been incorporated the much smaller Association Library and Amicable Library, was merged in 1769 into the Library Company. Duplicates—alas, any edition of the same title—were sold. The holdings and members of the two institutions were consolidated. A new printed catalogue with 2,033 entries was prepared and published in 1770. On this occasion the books were renumbered by size, beginning an accession series that continues to this day.

Women were never officially excluded from using the library. In her diary, Hannah Callendar mentioned visiting and using the Library Company in the 1750s and 1760s. She did not own a share, but her father did, and she is probably representative of a number of female family members who used the collection through their male relatives. The first official female shareholders are documented in 1769. Two of them, Sarah Emlen and Susanna Carmalt, joined when the Library

Bookplates of the Amicable Library, the Association Library, and the Union Library Company. These early subscription libraries were absorbed by the Library Company in 1769.

Company absorbed the Union Library Company in April, and on May 9, Sarah Wister was voted a share. Ann Bartram, daughter of the famous botanist William Bartram and herself an illustrator, was also an early member. It seems likely that there was some discussion among the directors about the admission of women into their ranks, but the Minute Books are silent on the issue. By the turn of the nineteenth century there were twenty-nine women shareholders, a number that would increase dramatically to nearly 800 by the end of the century.

In 1772, the library having "become large & valuable, a Source of Instruction to Individuals and conducive of Reputation to the Public," and much too crowded in its State House rooms, the directors petitioned the Pennsylvania Assembly for permission to build on the State House Square. The request was turned down. After much consideration and no alleviation of the space problem, agreement was reached with the Carpenters' Company in 1773 to rent the second floor of their new hall off Chestnut Street near Fourth. "The Books (inclosed within Wire Lattices) are kept in one large Room," Franklin, then in London, was informed, "and in another handsome Appartment the [scientific] Apparatus is deposited and the Directors meet."

It was a historic move. On September 5, 1774, the First Continental Congress met on the first floor of Carpenters' Hall. John Adams reported that the site committee had taken "a View of the Room, and of the Chamber where is an excellent Library." In anticipation of the meeting, the Library Company had ordered that "the Librarian furnish the Gentlemen who are to meet in Congress in this City with the use of such Books as they may have occasion for during their sitting taking a Receipt for them." The first day it met, Congress recorded the credentials of the delegates. On the second day it formally expressed its thanks for the Library Company's courtesy.

The offer of the use of the collections was renewed when the Second Continental Congress met the following spring and again when the delegates to the Constitutional Convention met in 1787. In fact, for a quarter of a century, from 1774 until the national capital was established in Washington, D.C., in 1800, the Library Company, long the most important book resource for colonial Philadelphians, served as the *de facto* Library of Congress before there was one *de jure*. Unfortunately, no circulation records for the period exist, so we can never know which delegate or congressman borrowed or consulted

United States, Continental Congress, *Journal of the Proceedings of Congress.* Philadelphia: William and Thomas Bradford, 1774. Gift of Owen Biddle, 1779.

JOURNAL

OF THE

PROCEEDINGS

OF THE

CONGRESS,

Held at PHILADELPHIA,
September 5, 1774.

PHILADELPHIA:
Printed by WILLIAM and THOMAS BRADFORD,
at the *London Coffee-House.*
M,DCC,LXXIV.

Thomas Hobbes, *Leviathan, Or the Matter, Forme and Power of a Commonwealth.* London, 1751. John Dickinson's copy.

George Nelson

COMMON SENSE;

ADDRESSED TO THE

INHABITANTS

OF

AMERICA,

On the following interesting

SUBJECTS.

I. Of the Origin and Design of Government in general, with concise Remarks on the English Constitution.

II. Of Monarchy and Hereditary Succession.

III. Thoughts on the present State of American Affairs.

IV. Of the present Ability of America, with some miscellaneous Reflections.

Man knows no Master save creating HEAVEN,
Or those whom choice and common good ordain.
THOMSON.

PHILADELPHIA;
Printed, and Sold, by R. BELL, in Third-Street.
MDCCLXXVI.

Thomas Paine, *Common Sense*.
Philadelphia: R. Bell, 1776.

Loan Slip for Common Sense.
Signed by George Walton,
Philadelphia, 1781.

I PROMISE to pay to the LIBRARY COMPANY of *Philadelphia*, or Order, the Sum of ———— for Value received. *Nevertheless*, if within ———— Weeks, from the Date hereof, I return, undefaced, to their *Librarian*, a Book belonging to the said *Library Company* of *Philadelphia*, intituled, ———— which I now have borrowed, this Bill is to be void. Witness my Hand, this ———— Day of ———— 1781.

Geo Walton.

what work. But virtually every significant work on political theory, history, law, and statecraft (and much else besides) could be found on the Library Company's shelves, along with numerous tracts and polemical writings by American as well as European authors. And virtually all of the works that influenced the minds of the Framers of the nation are still on the Library Company's shelves. It was said, although

Giuseppe Ceracchi, *Minerva as the Patroness of American Liberty*. Painted terra cotta, Philadelphia, 1791. This monumental sculpture loomed over the Speaker's chair in Congress Hall while the federal capital was in Philadelphia.

the records of neither Congress nor the Library Company contain any information to corroborate the story, that the colossal bust of Liberty made by Giuseppe Ceracchi, which stood behind the chair of the Speaker of the House in the late 1790s, was given to the Library Company as a token of thanks when the government left the city.

In 1775, at the time when he joined Dr. Johnson in opposing the actions of the colonies, the evangelical preacher John Wesley sent some books to the library; they were of a religious nature, not political polemics. In the months of growing turmoil the directors tried to continue normal procedures. Just when the news of Lexington and Concord reached Philadelphia, a supplement to the 1770 catalogue was delivered by Robert Aitken, who later also printed the "Bible of the Revolution." Nonetheless, the affairs of the Library Company were overwhelmed by events. On July 9, 1776, only two directors showed up for a meeting, and "no business was done." At the end of the year it was announced that books had to be obtained from the librarian's house because the first floor of Carpenters' Hall was being used as an infirmary for sick soldiers. The British occupation of the city also in-

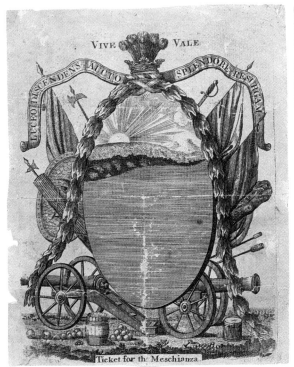

[John André], *Ticket for the Meschianza*. Philadelphia, May 18, 1778. Gift of Mrs. John M. Read, 1900.

[John André], *Sketch of a Meschianza Costume*. [Philadelphia, 1778]. Gift of John Fanning Watson, 1830. The Meschianza was an extravagant fete orchestrated by Major André for the British officers on the eve of their withdrawal from Philadelphia.

terrupted the routine; the directors did not meet between October 1777 and March 1778. After that, things seem to have gone on smoothly. Just before the British left, the Tory bookseller of New York, James Rivington, sent the library "all the Books to be procured at present in this place." Insofar as the Minutes reflect what was going on, the Library Company seemed insulated from the trials and successes of the new nation.

During the war years, importation of books from abroad had ceased. With the peace in 1783 a flurry of orders went to London agents Joseph Woods and William Dilwyn. The library's seriousness of purpose was reiterated when the directors told their correspondents that "tho we would wish to mix the *Utile* with the *Dulce*, we should not think it expedient to add to our present stock, anything in the *novel* way." It was with presumably unspent book funds that the Library Company in 1785 made what has proved to be the most valuable purchase in its history. At the sale of the effects of the Swiss-born would-be historian of America, Pierre Eugène Du Simitière, the Library Company was the main buyer, securing most of his manuscript collections and almost all the volumes of broadsides, prints, and pamphlets offered at the auction. Du Simitière, with an eye to the future, had picked up ephemera from the streets. An unbelievably high percentage of the printed items that he gathered is today unique, illuminating the Revolutionary era as only a period's informal productions can.

When the Reverend Manasseh Cutler visited Philadelphia in 1787, he paid his respects to the institution that had "become the public library of the University and City":

> Every modern author of any note, I am told, is to be met with here, and large additions are annually made. The books appeared to be well arranged and in good order. . . . I was pleased with a kind of network doors to the book-shelves,

[Benjamin Franklin], *Magna Britannia: Her Colonies Reduc'd.* [London, 1765–66]. Only known copy; Du Simitière Collection, 1785.

For SALE *at* PUBLIC VENDUE,

On THURSDAY the 10th Day of March, at the late Dwelling House of

Pierre Eugene du Simitiere, Esq.

In Arch-street, between Third and Fourth-streets, where the State Lottery Office is now kept,

THE AMERICAN MUSÆUM.

This curious Collection was, for many Years, the principal Object of Mr. Du Simitiere's Attention, and has been thought worthy of Notice by both American and European Literati: It consists of the following Articles, which will be sold in Lots, viz.

BOOKS.

LOT
1 ALMANACS and Registers

2 Architecture, viz.

3 Catalogues of Books and Curiosities.

4 Dictionaries and Grammars, viz.

5 Drawing, viz.

6 Divinity, viz.

7 Geography and Astronomy, viz.

8 Heraldry, viz.

9 History, viz.

10 Mathematics, viz.

11 Miscellany, (a) viz.

A Lot (b) consisting of

12 Occult Philosophy, viz.

13 Natural History, viz.

14 Physic and Surgery, viz.

15 Poetry, viz.

16 Voyages and Travels, viz.

17 Books and Papers relat. to America, viz.

18 News-Papers, viz.

COINS.

19 A Mahogany Cabinet containing ancient and modern Gold, Silver and Copper Coins and Medals; among which are some very curious Bronzes.

CURIOSITIES.

20 Indian and African Antiquities, Dresses, Weapons, Utensils, &c.

21 Preservations in Spirits, in 38 Phials.

22 An elegant Collection of Shells and other Marine Productions.

23 Fossils and Petrifactions.

24 A Collection of Woods, Barks, Fruits, Pods, &c. from the West-Indies.

DRAWINGS & PRINTS.

25 A Port Folio containing about 170 Drawings.

26 Ditto (a) containing about 240 Prints

27 Ditto (b) — 390 do.

28 Ditto (c) — 250 do.

29 Ditto (d) — 140 do.

30 Ditto (b) — 110 do.

31 Ditto (f) containing Drawings, finished and unfinished; Specimens of Writing and of old Print.

32 Ditto (g) containing about 170 Prints, and a Hortus Siccus.

33 Ditto (h) containing about 160 Maps and Plans.

HORTI SICCI.

34 A Port Folio (g)

35 Ditto

AMERICAN MONEY.

36 A Collection of Parchment and Paper Money.

MATTHEW CLARKSON, } Administrators.
EBENEZER HAZARD,

Philadelphia, printed by CHARLES CIST, at the Corner of Fourth and Arch-streets.

For Sale at Public Vendue. Philadelphia, [1785]. Broadside announcing the post-mortem sale of the Pierre Eugène Du Simitière Collection.

An ELEGIAC

POEM,

On the DEATH of that celebrated Divine, and eminent Servant of JESUS CHRIST, the late Reverend, and pious

GEORGE WHITEFIELD,

Chaplain to the Right Honourable the Countefs of HUNTINGDON, &c &c.

Who made his Exit from this tranfitory State, to dwell in the celeftial Realms of Blifs, on LORD's-Day, 30th of September, 1770, when he was feiz'd with a Fit of the Afthma, at NEWBURY-PORT, near BOSTON, in NEW-ENGLAND. In which is a Condolatory Addrefs to His truly noble Benefactrefs the worthy and pious Lady HUNTINGDON,---and the Orphan-Children in GEORGIA ; who, with many Thoufands, are left, by the Death of this great Man, to lament the Lofs of a Father, Friend, and Benefactor.

By PHILLIS, a Servant Girl of 17 Years of Age, belonging to Mr. J. WHEATLEY, of BOSTON :---And has been but 9 Years in this Country from Africa.

HAIL happy Saint on thy immortal throne !
   To thee complaints of grievance are unknown ;
We hear no more the mufic of thy tongue,
Thy wonted auditories ceafe to throng.
Thy leffons in unequal'd accents flow'd !
While emulation in each bofom glow'd ;
Thou didft, in ftrains of eloquence refin'd,
Inflame the foul, and captivate the mind.
Unhappy we, the fetting Sun deplore !
Which once was fplendid, but it fhines no more ;
He leaves this earth for Heaven's unmeafur'd height :
And worlds unknown, receive him from our fight ;
There WHITEFIELD wings, with rapid courfe his way,
And fails to Zion, through vaft feas of day.

   When his AMERICANS were burden'd fore,
When ftreets were crimfon'd with their guiltlefs gore !
Unrival'd friendfhip in his breaft now ftrove :
The fruit thereof was charity and love
Towards America-----couldft thou do more
Than leave thy native home, the Britifh fhore,
To crofs the great Atlantic's wat'ry road,
To fee America's diftrefs'd abode ?
Thy prayers, great Saint, and thy inceffant cries,
Have pierc'd the bofom of thy native fkies !
Thou moon haft feen, and ye bright ftars of light
Have witnefs been of his requefts by night !
He pray'd that grace in every heart might dwell :
He long'd to fee America excell ;
He charg'd its youth to let the grace divine
Arife, and in their future actions fhine ;
He offer'd THAT he did himfelf receive,

A greater gift not GOD himfelf can give :
He urg'd the need of HIM to every one ;
It was no lefs than GOD's co-equal SON !
Take HIM ye wretched for your only good ;
Take HIM ye ftarving fouls to be your food.
Ye thirfty, come to this life giving ftream :
Ye Preachers, take him for your joyful theme :
Take HIM, " my dear AMERICANS," he faid,
Be your complaints in his kind bofom laid :
Take HIM ye Africans, he longs for you ;
Impartial SAVIOUR, is his title due ;
If you will chufe to walk in grace's road,
You fhall be fons, and kings, and priefts to GOD.

   Great COUNTESS ! we Americans revere
Thy name, and thus condole thy grief fincere :
We mourn with thee, that TOMB obfcurely plac'd,
In which thy Chaplain undifturb'd doth reft.
New-England fure, doth feel the ORPHAN's fmart ;
Reveals the true fenfations of his heart :
Since this fair Sun, withdraws his golden rays,
No more to brighten thefe diftrefsful days !
His lonely Tabernacle, fees no more
A WHITEFIELD landing on the Britifh fhore :
Then let us view him in yon azure fkies :
Let every mind with this lov'd object rife.
No more can he exert his lab'ring breath,
Seiz'd by the cruel meffenger of death.
What can his dear AMERICA return ?
But drop a tear upon his happy urn,
Thou tomb, fhalt fafe retain thy facred truft,
Till life divine re-animate his duft,

Sold by EZEKIEL RUSSELL, in Queen-Street, and JOHN BOYLES, in Marlboro'-Street.

Phillis Wheatley, *An Elegiac Poem, on the Death of . . . George Whitefield.* [Boston, 1770]. Only known perfect copy; Du Simitière Collection, 1785.

MUSICIENS d'un CALINDA

Pierre Eugène Du Simitière, *Musiciens d'un Calinda*. Ink and wash drawing, Jamaica, ca. 1760. Du Simitière Collection, 1785.

which is made of a large wire sufficiently open to read the labels, but no book can be taken out unless the librarian unlocks the door. This is a necessary security from any persons taking books without the knowledge of the librarian. . . .

From the Library we were conducted into the Cabinet, which is a large room on the opposite side of the entry, and over the room where the Mechanical models are deposited [by the American Philosophical Society]. Here we had the pleasure of viewing a most excellent collection of natural curiosities from all parts of the globe.

Although the contents of the museum and the scientific instruments remained in the Library Company's possession for some time, gifts to the cabinet fell off. There is no record of the disposal of any of the items, but only a very few of them have survived.

There was an upsurge of optimism after the government was established under the Constitution. Growth had continued, and the library's rented quarters became inadequate. Negotiations with the legislature for ground and with the American Philosophical Society for some jointure of interest fell through. In 1789 the Library Company bought a piece of land on Fifth Street near Chestnut across from State House Square. A competition for the design of a building was held. An amateur architect, Dr. William Thornton, won it with plans for a handsome Palladian red-brick structure with white pilasters and a balustrade surmounted by urns. A curving double flight of steps led up

William Birch, *Library and Surgeon's Hall, Fifth-street*. Engraving, from *The City of Phiadelphia*. Philadelphia, 1800.

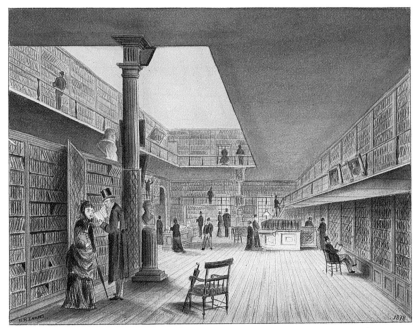

Benjamin Evans, *Interior of Phila; Library, Fifth and Library Streets*. Watercolor, 1878. One of 151 Evans drawings purchased in 1975.

Samuel Jennings, *Liberty Displaying the Arts and Sciences*. Oil on canvas, London, 1792. Gift of the artist.

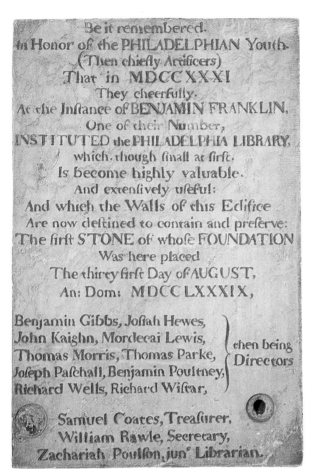

Be it remembered.
In Honor of the PHILADELPHIAN Youth.
(Then chiefly Artificers)
That in MDCCXXXI
They cheerfully.
At the Inſtance of BENJAMIN FRANKLIN,
One of their Number,
INSTITUTED the PHILADELPHIA LIBRARY,
which though ſmall at firſt.
Is become highly valuable.
And extenſively uſeful:
And which the Walls of this Edifice
Are now deſtined to contain and preſerve:
The firſt STONE of whoſe FOUNDATION
Was here placed
The thirty firſt Day of AUGUST,
An: Dom: MDCCLXXXIX,

Benjamin Gibbs, Joſiah Hewes,
John Kaighn, Mordecai Lewis,
Thomas Morris, Thomas Parke,   then being
Joſeph Paſchall, Benjamin Poultney,   Directors
Richard Wells, Richard Wiſtar,

Samuel Coates, Treaſurer,
William Rawle, Secretary,
Zachariah Poulſon, jun' Librarian.

Original Cornerstone of the Library Company's Building on Fifth Street, 1789.

to the frontispiece, over which, under a pronounced pediment, was an arched niche. This was filled by a gift from William Bingham: a statue of Franklin classically garbed in a toga—with his permission—carved out of marble in Italy by Francesco Lazzarini. The cornerstone, with an inscription composed by Franklin except for a flattering reference to him, was laid on August 31, 1789. He did not live to see the building finished. The new quarters were opened on New Year's Day, 1791. For the new library, Samuel Jennings, an expatriate Philadelphian living in London, painted a large picture, "Liberty Displaying the Arts and Sciences."

When the new library was in operation, conversations were held seeking an arrangement with the Loganian Library, housed on Sixth Street across the State House Square. James Logan, who had come to

Pennsylvania as William Penn's secretary in 1699 and in the course of years occupied many of the highest political and judicial offices of the province, was a bookman all his life. A linguist of competence in a bewildering number of languages, a classicist who in the margins of his books crossed swords with the greatest European editors, and a scientist who described the fertilization of corn by pollen, understood and used the new inventions of calculus, wrote on optics, and made astronomical observations, the Quaker virtuoso bought books to feed the wide-ranging appetite of his mind. By the time he died in 1751, Logan had gathered over 2,600 volumes, chiefly in Latin and Greek; it was the best collection of books in colonial America.

In his later years, Logan had decided to leave his books for the use of the public and established a library, an American Bodleian. He designed and began constructing the building to house it on Sixth Street

Thomas Sully, *James Logan*. Oil on canvas, Philadelphia, 1831. After an original by Gustavus Hesselius. Commissioned to replace a portrait lost by fire in 1831.

PHILOSOPHIÆ

NATURALIS

PRINCIPIA

MATHEMATICA.

Autore JS. NEWTON, Trin. Coll. Cantab. Soc. Matheseos Professore Lucasiano, & Societatis Regalis Sodali.

IMPRIMATUR·
S. PEPYS, Reg. Soc. PRÆSES.
Julii 5. 1686.

LONDINI,

Jussu Societatis Regiæ ac Typis Josephi Streater. Prostat apud plures Bibliopolas. Anno MDCLXXXVII.

Isaac Newton, *Philosophiæ Naturalis Principia Mathematica*. London, 1687.

James Logan, *Difficiliorum quorundam Elucidatio*. Manuscript explanations of certain of Newton's propositions tipped into the front of Logan's copy of the *Principia*.

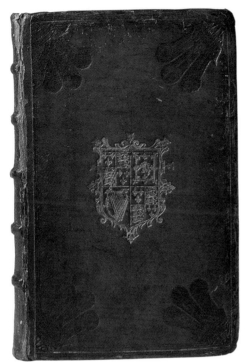

Geoffrey Chaucer, *Works*. London, 1602. James Logan's copy, originally bound for Henry, Prince of Wales, with his arms and feather insignia.

and wrote an elaborate codicil to his will setting up the institution and endowing it with the rents of a property in Bucks County. The original trustees had included his son-in-law, Isaac Norris, Jr., but as a result of a disagreement with him, Logan canceled the codicil. He intended to frame another instrument, but illness prevented him from perfecting it. Nonetheless, after his death his heirs carried out the old

Loganian Library. Ink and wash drawing, [1797?].

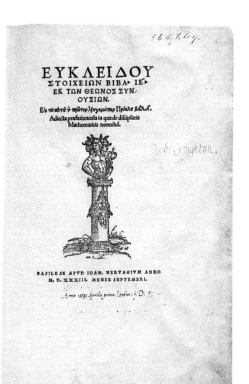

Euclid, *Works*. Basel, 1533.
Given to the Loganian Library
in 1776 by William Logan of
Bristol. Inscribed in 1553 by
John Dee, first English translator
of Euclid.

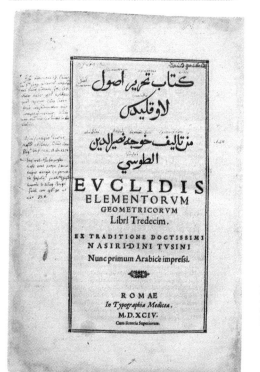

Euclid in Arabic. Rome, 1594.
James Logan's copy, with notes
in his Arabic handwriting.

man's wishes. The Loganian Library was created in 1754 as a trust for the public with Logan's sons, William and James, his son-in-law John Smith, Benjamin Franklin, Richard Peters, Israel Pemberton, Jr., and William Allen as trustees. A second deed of trust, almost identical to the earlier one, was dated March 25, 1760.

A printed catalogue of the Bibliotheca Loganiana, prepared by Lewis Weiss, a German immigrant, was issued in 1760, the year the library was opened. Although Franklin, in his promotional tract for the establishment of a college in Philadelphia, had described Logan's library as a valuable book resource available to professors and students, use was seldom made of the collection's scholarly works. In the eighteenth century, merchants and artisans in Philadelphia had little interest in the classics and advanced mathematical sciences. Moreover, two factors that made Logan's library unique contributed to its unpopularity; it included few English works of *belles lettres* and, at the opposite pole, almost no polemical theology or politics.

In 1758, Dr. William Logan, a physician of Bristol, England, and the younger brother of James, died without issue and left much of his estate, including his library, to his nephew William Logan of Philadelphia. Dr. William Logan's books included a high proportion of medical works, and in pre-Revolutionary days it may have been the largest and best—albeit somewhat old-fashioned—such collection in the colonies. When the American William Logan died in 1776, he left from his inheritance such books as did not duplicate titles in the Loganian Library to that institution and the duplicates to the Library Company.

When the handsome Library Company building began to rise across the square from the Loganian Library, James Logan, Jr., the sole survivor of the original trustees, asked the General Assembly of Pennsylvania to vest the trust in the Library Company to make his father's benefaction more useful. By an act of March 31, 1792, the books and assets of the Loganian Library were transferred into the custody of the far more active institution. An addition to its just completed building was quickly erected as an east wing. There were almost 4,000 volumes in the Loganian Library, which, after being moved into new quarters, were listed in a new catalogue published in 1795. The weightiness in pounds and in contents can be judged from the fact that almost one-quarter of the total number of volumes were in folio size.

Thomas Sully, *Zachariah Poulson, Jr.*
Oil on canvas, Philadelphia, 1843.
Librarian from 1785 to 1806.
Commissioned from the artist.

A succession of functionaries of brief incumbency, including John Todd, Jr., who later became the first husband of Dolley Madison, handled the operation of the library until Zachariah Poulson, Jr. became the librarian in 1785. Poulson was a printer, newspaper publisher, and excellent keeper of books and records. He compiled and printed an indexed catalogue in 1789, kept admirable accounts of books borrowed, and set up "A Chronological Register" of shares that retrospectively listed the original and successive owners of each share from 1731 on. The register has been kept up and is still in use. Each librarian was held personally responsible for the integrity of the collection, and inventories were taken when one resigned or was replaced to determine how much should be charged him for loss during his incumbency. This amount was sometimes waived; it was frequently uncollectible.

The number of shareholders had reached 100 in 1763 and remained at that level until the merger with the Union Library in 1769, when it jumped to 400. To pay for the Fifth Street building, 266 shares were sold or given to the carpenters, bricklayers, and others in 1789–1793 in partial payment for work done. The cost of a share was increased in 1793 from £20 fluctuating Pennsylvania money to $40 in good Hamiltonian currency, and the annual dues were set at $2. Thereafter, growth was gradual, the membership rising to over 800 in the 1820s. Both members and nonmembers paid a fee for taking out books, but anyone was permitted to read in the library without charge. Penalties were levied for keeping books out overlong.

Poulson, who was responsible for getting the operational affairs of the institution on a workmanlike basis, served as librarian for over two decades. On December 3, 1801, in appreciation of the director's commendation of his services up to that time, he gave the library ten folio, thirty-seven quarto, and four octavo volumes of miscellaneous pamphlets, chiefly from the seventeenth century. These added over 1,000 titles to the Library Company's holdings. The number in itself was important, but it was far outweighed by the comparatively recent discovery that all these volumes had belonged to Benjamin Franklin.

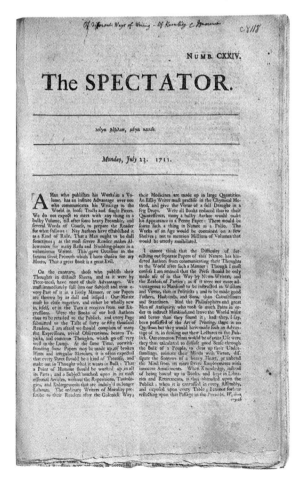

The Spectator. London, 1711. Franklin's copy; gift of Zachariah Poulson, Jr., 1801. Franklin taught himself to write by copying the style of this English periodical.

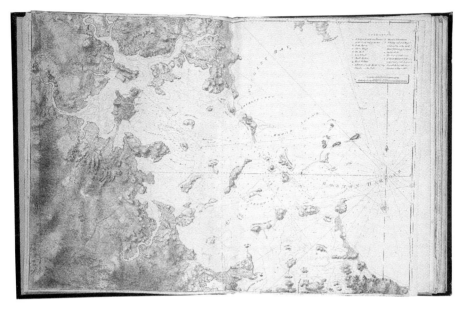

Joseph Frederick Wallet Des Barres, *The Atlantic Neptune*. [London, 1777]. This atlas was taken as a prize from a British brig and was used by the Continental Congress during the Revolution. Gift of Joseph Parker Norris, 1824.

Poulson's gift represents almost half of the 2,150 titles on the Library Company's shelves that once belonged to Franklin.

The library's role in the life of Philadelphia was maintained. It was, and remained until late in the nineteenth century, "the City Library" or the "the Philadelphia Library." Citizens of prominence were its members. Nine signers of the Declaration of Independence— Benjamin Franklin, Benjamin Rush, Francis Hopkinson, Robert Morris, George Clymer, John Morton, James Wilson, Thomas McKean, and George Ross—owned shares, and some of them served as directors. At the turn of the century those who were most active in the management of the Library Company were Richard Wells, Benjamin R. Morgan, William Rawle, Joseph Parker Norris, Robert Waln, and Samuel M. Fox, all of whom were leaders or participants in the civic and philanthropic activities of the city. They saw that the library's finances were properly managed and that orders for books were sent regularly to London agents and, after the semiannual shipments were carefully checked, paid for. Local booksellers and publishers were also patronized, but it was the important works from abroad—novels by Sir Walter Scott and Charlotte Smith, poetry by Lord Byron, accounts of Napoleon and his wars, and descriptions of travels to the still "new worlds" of Africa and Asia—for which the Library Company was justly renowned. Philadelphia printers borrowed the English imports and used and abused them to such an extent that a by-law was passed in 1805 declaring that printers would be sued if they took the Library Company's books apart in the course of reprinting the work. The same problem recurred in the second half of the twentieth century.

In addition to gifts of their own works by member-authors such as Charles Brockden Brown, a number of interesting accessions flowed into the library. In 1788, as secretary of the Pennsylvania Society for the Abolition of Slavery, Tench Coxe, later Hamilton's assistant in the Treasury Department, placed in the Library Company a handful of an-

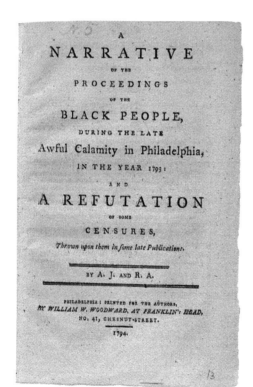

Absalom Jones and Richard Allen, *Narrative of the Proceedings of the Black People*. Philadelphia, 1794. Gift of the authors, 1794.

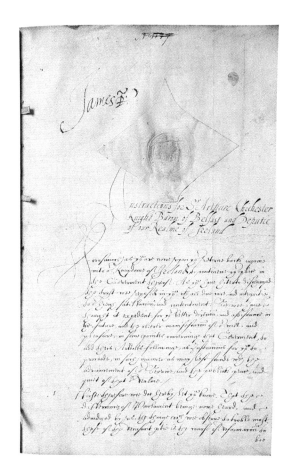

James I, *Instructions for Sr Arthure Chicester*. Manuscript on vellum, Greenwich, June 5, 1614. Gift of Henry Cox, 1799.

tislavery pamphlets sent to the Society from England and France, remarking that he knew of no depository "so proper" for such material.

In March 1799, the directors were surprised to receive, as a gift from a stranger, Henry Cox of Ireland, a black box containing a number of books, manuscripts, and printed records. They had come down to him from his grandfather, Sir Richard Cox, Lord Chancellor of Ireland in 1703–1707, who had appropriated them. When William Hepworth Dixon, a British historian, saw the manuscripts in Philadelphia in 1866, he recognized them as part of the official Irish archives and suggested that they were of such paramount importance that they should be returned to Great Britain. The directors agreed and formally offered to Lord Romilly, Master of the Rolls, several of the manuscripts containing correspondence between James I and the Privy Council of Ireland, orders of the Council, and the diary and letterbook of the

Marquis of Clanricarde, Lord Deputy of Ireland. The offer was gratefully accepted. In return, the Library Company was given several series of British government publications of an antiquarian nature. Of greater import, however, was the discovery thirty years later of the "Mayflower Compact," which was generously sent back to Massachusetts by Queen Victoria's officials. *The Times* noted, "The precedent of the Library Company of Philadelphia . . . has unquestionably played a considerable part in determining the action of the Consistory Court." Inexplicably, the directors did not return a number of other valuable documents from the same source, including James I's original instructions of 1614 to his Lord Deputy of Ireland, Sir Arthur Chichester, and some dozens of unique seventeenth-century Irish broadsides.

A far larger gift came as the bequest in 1803 of the Reverend Dr. Samuel Preston, rector of Chevening in Kent. It is not known exactly why he chose the Library Company to be the recipient of his book bounty. In 1783, Preston, an ardent Whig, had written to the direc-

Benjamin West, *The Reverend Samuel Preston, of Chevening in Kent*. Oil on canvas, 1797. Gift of Preston's widow, 1803.

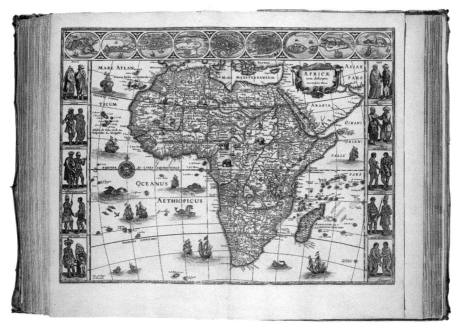

Willem Janzoon and Jan Blaeu, *Le Theatre Du Monde Ou Nouvel Atlas*. Amsterdam, 1644–46. Samuel Preston bequest, 1803.

tors congratulating them on the exploits of their fellow countrymen and wishing the Library Company well in the days to come, and in 1784 he sent the Library Company a copy of the two-volume folio Hebrew Old Testament prepared by the erudite Benjamin Kennicott because, he said, of the "high regard I have ever entertained for the People of America, particularly those of the Province of Pennsylvania." Preston may have met Franklin during the latter's visit to Chevening in August 1774. Nicholas Biddle later related that the American artist Benjamin West, who painted Preston's portrait in 1797, "induced Preston to give his valuable library to Phila." In any event, the Preston bequest consisted of over 2,500 volumes, the lifetime accumulation of a well-to-do, cultured gentleman cleric. It included an appropriate proportion of theological works but was also rich in handsome and expensive works of geography, history, and the fine arts. When the books arrived in America, Congress refused to remit the duties, which were grudgingly paid.

The library's next major accession was in 1828 upon the death of the Philadelphia merchant William Mackenzie. Little is known of the

John Neagle, *William Mackenzie*.
Oil on canvas, 1829. After an
original, now lost, given by
Dr. James Abercrombie in 1828.

Caius Plinius Secundus,
Historia Naturale. Venice:
Nicolas Jenson, 1476.
Mackenzie bequest, 1828.

man except that he was wealthy, generous, and a true bibliophile. Mackenzie was the first American to collect books for the sake of their rarity, their age, or their beauty, gathering them together from every part of Europe and America. He was, in short, America's first rare book collector. He acquired such "collectors' items" as Jacobus de Voragine's *Golden Legende* printed by Caxton in 1438, Jenson's 1476 Italian Pliny on vellum, and many French books, from romances of chivalry to Oudry's rococo masterpiece, La Fontaine's *Fables Choisies* (Paris, 1755–1759). In addition to rarities, among them dozens of pamphlets of the Revolutionary period and other extremely valuable pieces of Americana, Mackenzie purchased the books of his day as they

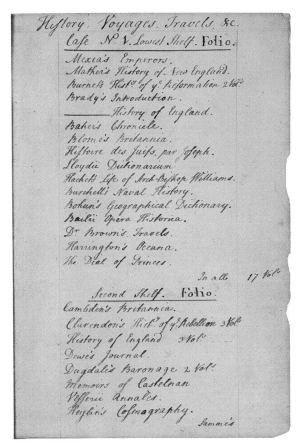

William Byrd, *A Catalogue of Books, in the Library at Westover*. Manuscript, ca. 1751. William Mackenzie bequest, 1828.

were published, and he bought heavily when important libraries were dispersed locally. As a result he was a major customer of the bookseller Nicholas Gouin Dufief in 1801–1803 when the collections of Benjamin Franklin and William Byrd of Westover were broken up and sold piecemeal. By his will, Mackenzie left all his pre-1700 books to the Loganian Library (which since 1792 had been consolidated with the Library Company) as well as another 800 volumes that the Loganian trustees could select from his French and Latin works. These amounted to 1,519 volumes; an additional 3,566 volumes were purchased on most favorable terms by the Loganian trustees from Mackenzie's executors. At the same time the Library Company acquired 1,966 volumes, mostly books in English. Thus Mackenzie's entire collection of over 7,000 books found its way into the Library Company.

In 1832, two other large libraries were added to the book resources of the Library Company. After the death of Zaccheus Collins, an amateur naturalist and longtime director of the library, the administrator

Hortus Sanitatis. Strassburg, 1497. Collins Collection, 1832.

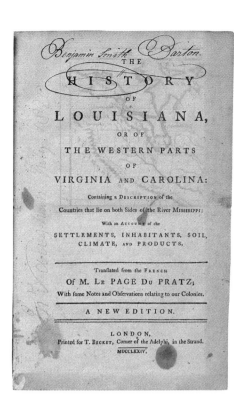

Antoine Simon Le Page Du Pratz, *The History of Louisiana*. London, 1774. Purchased 1823 at the sale of the library of Benjamin Smith Barton. Barton previously lent this copy to Meriwether Lewis, who took it on the famous expedition.

Inscription on fly-leaf by Meriwether Lewis, Philadelphia, May 7, 1807.

Mark Catesby, *The Natural History of Carolina, Florida, and the Bahama Islands*. London, 1771. Purchased 1772.

of his estate offered his books for sale. For $1,200 the collection, rich in works of botany and other fields of natural history, was purchased for the Loganian Library. Collins's books complemented the Library Company's already significant holdings in the field of natural history, for the Library Company was founded just as the Linnaean revolution was inspiring the first systematic classification of new American species of plants and animals. Many of the early naturalists were associated with the Library Company—John Bartram, James Logan, Peter Collinson, and Joseph Breintnall—and many other members at least dabbled in this exciting new field. One of the first books placed on the library's shelves was Philip Miller's *Gardener's Dictionary*, the gift of Peter Collinson. Mark Catesby's *Natural History of Carolina*, the first great color plate book of American natural history, was snapped up when a new edition was published in 1771.

The second major collection to come to the Library Company in 1832 was that of James Cox. He was an artist who had emigrated from London shortly after the Revolution. By chance, near his house on Almond Street in Philadelphia he met a woman who came from his own native village in England and who befriended him and made him her heir. When the lady died, Cox came into a modest fortune, enabling him to buy books and more books, which he did to the exclusion of all but the necessities of life. An eccentric bibliomaniac, he filled his house to overflowing with an accumulation of about 6,000 volumes, chiefly of a literary nature, including a first edition of Keats's *Poems*, which he seems to have bought when it was first published. A solitary octogenarian, overwhelmed by the size of his collection, Cox agreed in 1832 to give it to the Library Company in return for an annuity of $400. Two years later, Cox died; his library proved to be a most unusual bargain.

Joshua Shaw, *Picturesque Views of American Scenery*. Philadelphia, 1820. From the library of James Cox, 1834.

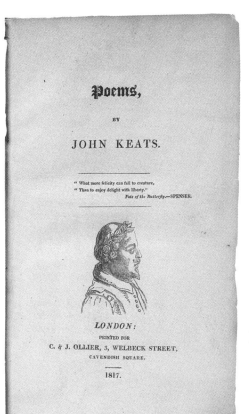

John Keats, *Poems*. London: C. Richards, 1817. From the library of James Cox, 1834.

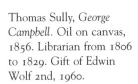

Thomas Sully, *George Campbell*. Oil on canvas, 1856. Librarian from 1806 to 1829. Gift of Edwin Wolf 2nd, 1960.

James Reid Lambdin,
John Jay Smith. Oil on
canvas, date unknown.
Librarian from 1829 to
1850. Gift of the Smith
family, 1883.

In 1806, Zachariah Poulson resigned as librarian and was succeeded
by George Campbell, who remained in office until 1829. These were
the days of printed catalogues. Supplements came out regularly; a new
"complete" listing was published in 1803; a Loganian supplement was
issued in 1828; and then, of course, the addition of the Mackenzie
books called forth another catalogue. In the spring of 1829, John Jay
Smith was elected librarian. He was a man of broad culture and considerable energy, with a host of extracurricular activities such as the
editing of a periodical, the promotion of Laurel Hill Cemetery, the
practice of landscape gardening, and the collection of family and other
early Pennsylvania manuscripts, which he eventually gave to the
Library Company. He was a descendant of James Logan through
Logan's daughter Hannah and was proud of his ancestry. Through no
fault of his, the only fire in the long history of the Library Company
occurred early in Smith's incumbency. On January 6, 1831, heat from
the fireplace in the Loganian room kindled a wooden beam hidden
beneath a veneer of masonry. Before it was extinguished, some of the

315

Fire Insurance Company ought to pay to the Library Company the amount of damage to maps $25 and the value of the large print and plan of the Siege of Gibralter $20. but that they ought not to pay for the Clock or the Bust of William Penn.

Feby 26. 1831.   Signed H. Binney

Amount of Loss by the fire at the Library on the 6th Jany 1831 exhibited to American Fire Insurance Company.

Recapitulation	Folio	Quarto	Octavo	Duo	Total		
Destroyed	24	74	78	66	292		
To be Rebound	182	242	490	489	1403		
Repaired	11	10	18	119	158		
Value Destroyed	$92	233.50	237.37	17.25	704.62		
Amt of Damage	247.75	181.25	207.61	182.37	819 -	$1523	12½
Clock Destroyed $200. Damage to maps						225	
Portrait of Logan $100. Bust of Penn 50						150	
Large Print of Sortie before Gibralter						20	
Expenses of Mr J. Smith for bill $167.09							
Appraisers Bill			80.00			247	09
Total damages & expenses to be paid						$2165	21
by the Insurance Company not including the Expenses of rebinding an estimate of which was Submitted herewith at						1375	43
						$3540	64
Not allowed $350. Charges 247. 09						597	09
Nett loss received						$2943	55

A letter was read from Mr James Cox, over

Minute Book. Philadelphia, March 1831. Lists the number and value of books affected by the fire on January 6, 1831.

contiguous woodwork caught fire, and a clock, the portrait of Logan, a bust of Penn, and some books were destroyed. The loss, covered by insurance, was not as great as was feared at first. Few books were a total loss, some had their edges scorched, and 1,403 volumes were rebound because their spines had been damaged.

A major catalogue of the Library Company's books, arranged by subject, was issued in 1835, followed two years later by one of the Loganian Library. These, with their supplements of 1856 and 1867, remained the library's basic finding aids for over a century. Statistics were then printed showing that in the two collections there were 25,684 works in 43,884 volumes. In 1845, Smith noted that the number of books in the building had doubled in the sixteen years of his administration, and "with the rapid multiplication of books in America, importations from England & the Continent, &c." he foresaw another doubling in the next twenty years. A new building was considered in 1846, and John Notman actually drew plans for it, but nothing came of that. Growing pains continued. When Charles Jewett published the first comprehensive survey of American libraries in 1851, the Library Company was one of only five institutions with as many as 50,000 volumes. The others were Harvard and Yale (both inclusive of their specialized graduate school collections), the Library of Congress, and the Boston Athenaeum. Only Harvard had more than the Library Company's approximate count of 60,000 volumes.

After more than two decades as librarian, John Jay Smith resigned in 1851, and his son, Lloyd Pearsall Smith, succeeded him. He was more of a classicist than his predecessors and was known for his wit and his judicious spicing of conversation with Latin tags. "*Custos librorum nascitur, non fit,*" he once wrote (translation: "Librarians are born, not made"). Lloyd P. Smith was also the first to look upon librarianship as a career.

The library continued to grow. Smith noted in 1856 that the majority of the 18,000 volumes added since the appearance of the 1835

TWO LINES GREAT PRIMER ROMAN.

Quousque tandem abutere, Catilina, patientia nostra? quamdiu nos etiam furor iste tuus eludet? quem ad finem sese effrenata jactabit au-ABCDEFGHIJKLMNOPQRST 1234567890

Archibald Binney and James Ronaldson, *Specimen of Printing Types*. [Philadelphia], 1812. The publisher Mathew Carey's copy; gift of Isaac Lea, ca. 1850.

Walt Whitman, *Leaves of Grass*. Brooklyn, New York, 1855. First edition, purchased 1855.

catalogue had been purchased with the members' annual payments. The quality and comprehensiveness of the library acquisitions were maintained: a little bit of the best of everything but an emphasis on history, biography, and travel, with a slowly increasing incursion of novels onto the shelves. American and foreign best-sellers, fiction and nonfiction, were ordered as a matter of course, but it is doubtful that any other library had the imagination—or the boldness—to buy when they were first published the little-regarded *Moby Dick* by Herman Melville and Walt Whitman's *Leaves of Grass*. The Library Company did.

Concern about the inadequacy of the Fifth Street building increased apace with acquisitions. "Subscriptions for the erection of a Fire-Proof Building for the Library" were sought. (The destruction of much of the Library of Congress made many institutions fire-conscious.) By 1869 a substantial fund, including a legacy of almost $50,000 from Joseph Fisher, had been raised. Some lots were purchased in an attempt to assemble sufficient ground at the corner of Juniper and Locust Streets.

P. S. Duval & Son after James Queen, *Buildings of the Great Central Fair, in Aid of the U. S. Sanitary Commission, Logan Square.* Lithograph, 1864. Gift of John A. McAllister, 1886.

William Penn's William and Mary Secretary Desk. England, ca. 1700. Displayed at the Great Central Fair, 1864. Gift of John Jay Smith, 1873.

who had just joined the staff, and Smith's aged father. A map was set up in the reading room with colored pins to show the changing positions of the armies as campaigns ebbed and flowed. When the Great Central Fair was held in 1864 on Logan Square, the Library Company lent such historic items as William Penn's desk and clock and some of its rarest books for exhibition. With money scarce, prices high, and many of the members in the army, it took all of Smith's ingenuity to maintain the currency of the book purchases, which were increasingly being dominated by a demand for novels by such popular, now almost-forgotten authors as Ellen Price Wood, Lady Blessington, and Mayne Reid, as well as French texts by the prolific Alexandre Dumas and George Sand.

In 1869, Dr. James Rush died. He was the son of the physician-patriot Benjamin Rush and husband and heir of Phoebe Ann Ridgway Rush, who had inherited a portion of her father Jacob Ridgway's immense fortune and had predeceased her husband. They were childless. In accordance with his will as presented to the directors of the Library Company by Henry J. Williams, Rush's brother-in-law, sole executor, and long-time director of the Library Company, Rush left an estate of nearly a million dollars to the Library Company—under certain conditions. The original will had been drawn up in 1860, and in the remaining years of his life, Dr. Rush added codicil upon codicil until he succeeded in obscuring his own somewhat eccentric wishes in a fog of words and admonitory clauses.

Anna C. Peale, *Jacob Ridgway*, *James Rush*, and *Phoebe Anne Ridgway Rush*. Oils on canvas, 1829. James Rush bequest, 1869.

His original intention was clear. With his money the Library Company was to purchase a plot of adequate size "situate between Fourth and Fifteenth and Spruce and Race Streets" and there build a "fire-proof building sufficiently large to accommodate and contain all the books of the Library Company of Philadelphia . . . and to provide for its future extension." He did not want anything fancy. Matters, however, were not permitted to rest there. In his second codicil, Dr. Rush authorized his executor, at his discretion, to do whatever he thought fit. Mr. Williams asserted that on his deathbed, Dr. Rush had expressed his specific desire that the library be built on a lot at Broad and Christian Streets, toward the purchase of which he had made a payment. The executor announced his intention of carrying out the testator's last oral wishes.

Dr. Rush, who was a studious, somewhat misanthropic, and definitely eccentric gentleman, set forth a number of curious stipulations and precatory provisions in his will, but he had a clear idea of what he wanted the Library Company, where he had spent many quiet, happy hours, to be. He wrote:

> I know that an ostentatious library to keep up with the progress of our country, collecting too many books, may be like an avaricious man who accumulates money to the ruin of both his modesty and his intellect.
>
> Let [the library] rest in a modest contentment in the useful quality of its volumes for the benefit, not the amusement alone of the public, nor let it over an ambitious store of inferior printed paper, flap its flimsy leaves, and crow out the highest number of worthless books. Let it be a favor for the eminent works of fiction to be found upon the shelves; but let it not keep cushioned seats for time-wasting and lounging readers, nor place for every-day novels, mind-tainting reviews, controversial politics, scribblings of poetry and prose, biographies of unknown names, nor for those teachers of disjointed thinking, the daily newspapers, except, perhaps for reference to support, since such an authority could never prove, the authentic date of an event. In short, let the managers think only of the intrinsic value of additions to their shelves.

While such an opinion of the printed word would not have reflected the tastes of the membership at large and while other stipulations were somewhat aggravating, it was Williams's firm decision to build the new library in South Philadelphia, both physically and psychologically removed from the homes and businesses of the members, that aroused the most opposition. At a meeting in October 1869 the membership voted to "accept the legacy of Dr. James Rush according to the terms expressed in his will," with 378 of the 969 members abstaining, 298 voting in favor of the resolution, and 293 voting against it. The members voted down a purely polite corollary motion expressing their gratitude for the bequest and their willingness to unite with Mr. Williams to carry out Dr. Rush's philanthropic intentions. A subsequently passed vote of thanks did nothing to placate Mr. Williams.

The directors of the Library Company were torn between a desire to benefit from the million-dollar bequest and their disapproval of Williams's plans for the site and the building. After several years, much bitterness, and a number of lawsuits, the huge Parthenon-like structure designed by Addison Hutton was erected at Broad and Christian Streets. In 1878 the Library Company reluctantly accepted the impressive edifice, which was named the Ridgway Library in honor of

The Ridgway Building, Broad and Christian Streets. Ca. 1940.

Interior of the Ridgway Building. Ca. 1940.

the original source of the funds that made it possible and the Rush bequest. The reader-members, however, had no intention of going down to South Philadelphia to browse or pick up the latest novels and biographies bought for the library.

By the time the Ridgway Library was completed, plans energetically forwarded by Henry Wharton, William Henry Rawle, and John S. Newbold were well advanced for another building at Juniper and Locust Streets, a location that was more central and more convenient for most of the members. Indeed, 692 of the 950 members were then living in town west of Tenth Street. The directors decided to use the Ridgway Library as a kind of storage house, although they never phrased it so crudely. They proceeded to relieve the crowded shelves on Fifth Street by moving to Broad Street "such books as, if destroyed by fire, could never be replaced" as well as all the Loganian books included in the 1837 catalogue. Frank Furness, a popular architect who favored the use of bricks to create his individualistic kind of Victorian eclecticism, designed the in-town library, where more modern books

Frank Furness. *Juniper and Locust Street Building.* Ink and wash drawing, ca. 1879.

would be housed and the main lending aspect of the Library Company could be conducted. On February 24, 1880, the new Juniper and Locust Street library opened its doors. Soon afterward, the Fifth Street property was sold.

In acknowledgment of the increasing number of women who became members throughout the nineteenth century, the plans for the Juniper and Locust Street building included a ladies' sitting room. The Library Company also hired its first woman librarian, Elizabeth McClellan, who had charge of the Women's Room (and attended exclusively to the wants of female readers) from 1880 until her death in 1920. (Because of the separate accommodations at the Juniper and Locust Street building, attendance records were kept by gender. They indicate that in the late nineteenth century, attendance of female and male shareholders was almost equal.)

Lloyd P. Smith, in whose home the plans for the first meeting of the projected American Library Association took place, was proud of his two "fire-proof" buildings. As one of the leaders in the new movement

Women's Room of the Juniper and Locust Street Building. From George Maurice Abbot, A *Short History of the Library Company of Philadelphia.* Philadelphia, 1913.

to professionalize librarianship, he wrote articles for the *Library Journal,* gave papers at meetings of the association, went with his peers to an international meeting in England, and developed a classification system for the shelving of the books in the two new buildings. The system used A for theology, E for jurisprudence, I for science and arts, O for literature, U for history and biography, and Y for bibliography, with lowercase letters and numerals for divisions and subdivisions of the categories. Within these subject classifications the books were shelved by size—folios, quartos, octavos, and duodecimos—and then by accession number.

This might have presented no problem had not the holdings of the Library Company been fragmented. The Library Company's old books were housed in the north wing of the Ridgway Library; the Loganian Library's old books were ranged on the balcony that ran around the huge, open reading room; the Library Company's new books were in the uptown library. Each collection was arranged separately according to the Smith system, and as new collections came into the library, each

The Revolution.

PRINCIPLE, NOT POLICY; JUSTICE, NOT FAVORS.

VOL. I.—NO. 1.   NEW YORK, WEDNESDAY, JANUARY 8, 1868. $2.00 A YEAR.

The Revolution, Vol. 1, No. 1 (January 8, 1868). Inscribed to Lucretia Mott from Susan B. Anthony. Gift of Edward W. Davis, 1883.

of them was also separately arranged. Duplicate catalogues and accession books had to be maintained for the two sites, for only the accession numbers appeared in the printed catalogues and on the handwritten paper slips that were used after 1857. These slips became the basis for the first, or possibly the second, card catalogue available for public use in an American library. (Though long since superseded, the catalogue still exists.) The method was ponderous, but for the 100,000 volumes that the Library Company had, according to a government survey of 1876, it worked. Although a new shelving method was introduced in 1953, some of the library is still arranged according to Smith's system.

James Reid Lambdin, *Lloyd Pearsall Smith*. Oil on canvas, date unknown. Librarian from 1851 to 1886. Gift of L. M. Smith, 1915.

Handwritten Cards from the Original Card Catalogue. After 1856.

Frederick Catherwood, *Views of Ancient Monuments*. London, 1844. James Rush bequest, 1869.

    The first considerable new accessions after the occupation of the Ridgway Library were the library and papers of Dr. James Rush that were part of his bequest. These included almost all the books of his celebrated father Benjamin Rush (probably the largest and best medical collection in the United States at the time of his death in 1813) and the manuscripts of many of his writings and lectures, notebooks, ledgers, medical records, and letters received. James Rush's own books and papers were far from inconsequential. His interests ranged from the valuable reference material that he had accumulated for the studies he wrote on the human voice and the human intellect to expensive, illustrated books on art, architecture, and antiquities.

    After the Civil War the position of the Library Company and of similar American subscription libraries was gradually but inexorably altered. The challenge came first from the mechanics' libraries, which provided reading material for workingmen, and then from the universities and the newly organized free public libraries, which grew rapidly in size, displacing the private subscription libraries as a community's

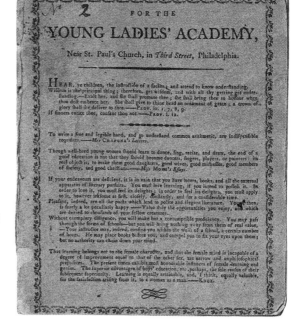

Benjamin Rush, *Manuscript Journal*. Page for November 1790 listing fees charged various patients, including the family of Vice President John Adams. James Rush bequest, 1869.

[Benjamin Rush], *For the Young Ladies' Academy*. Printed cover of an exercise book, 1787. James Rush bequest, 1869.

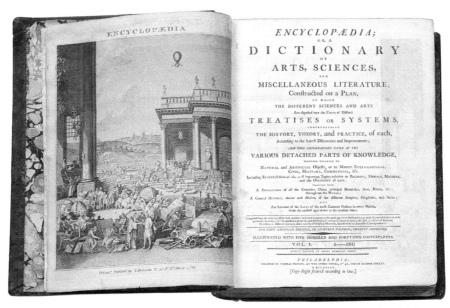

Thomas Dobson, *Encylopædia; Or, A Dictionary of Arts and Sciences*. Philadelphia: Thomas Dobson, 1798–1802. Benjamin Rush's copy, James Rush bequest, 1869.

John Moran, *Nos. 114 & 116 North Water St. 1868*, from *A Collection of Photographic Views in Philadelphia & Its Vicinity*. Albumen print photograph, 1868. Purchased from the photographer, 1870.

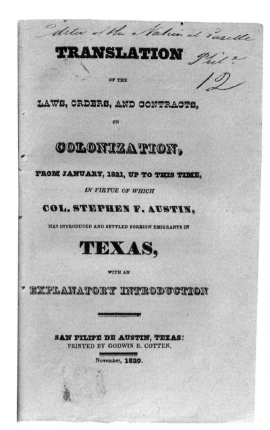

Stephen Fuller Austin, *Translation of the Laws, Orders, and Contracts, on Colonization.* San Filipe De Austin, Texas, November, 1829. Purchased at the sale of the library of Henry D. Gilpin, 1878.

principal repository of books. The Library Company noticed that far more nonmembers than members were beginning to use its resources. Subscribers without voting privileges could pay a fee for the right to borrow books. A recognition of the changing times impelled Dr. S. Weir Mitchell, author and physician, to suggest in 1886 that a study be made "to consider whether it may not be possible to make of the Philadelphia Library a Library free to all." The historian of the inquisition, Henry C. Lea, certainly had that concept in mind when he gave $50,000 to enlarge the library building, conditioning his gift upon the Library Company's agreement "not at any future time to abridge the privileges heretofore so liberally extended to the public."

At the same time the library's potential scholarly resources grew impressively. In 1884 the chess library of Professor George Allen—said at the time to have been the fifth finest collection of its kind in the world—was bought. Late that year, Margaretta A. Dick donated a col-

God connected the creation of man with the future creation of Christ in the human nature. — The enemy in the form of the serpent tried to defeat this.

Die viero figur.

[Stephan Fridolin], *Das Büch der Schatzbehalter*. Nuremberg, 1491. Purchased 1878.

Chess Automaton. Allen Chess collection, 1884.

lection of books, chiefly Americana and many editions of the *Book of Common Prayer,* which she had purchased for $1,000 from the estate of John McAllister. A year and a half later, his son, John A. McAllister, owner of the city's leading optical supply house and an incorrigible magpie, gave the Library Company his comprehensive pickings of a lifetime. He mounted these in dozens of folio scrapbooks of prints, photographs, playbills, political cartoons, paper currency, songsheets,

John A. McAllister, *Scrapbook.* Gift of John A. McAllister, 1886.

Mah.has.kah, Chief of
the Ioways.(White cloud).

Cephas Grier Childs,
*Mah-has-kah, Chief of
the Ioways—(White
Cloud)*. Colored
lithograph,
[Philadelphia, 1830].
Gift of John A.
McAllister, 1884. A
trial proof, never
used, intended for
Thomas L. McKenney
and James Hall, *History
of the Indian Tribes of
North America*.

broadsides, newspaper clippings, letters, and memorabilia of all kinds.
The Civil War period was covered exhaustively. The directors, expressing appreciation of the gift, commented that the collection "cannot fail to be of interest to the student of this period of the history of
our country." To McAllister is owed the preservation of many once lit-
tle-valued printed trifles of the nineteenth century. McAllister was also
responsible for convincing Charles A. Poulson, son of Zachariah
Poulson, Jr., to donate his extensive collection of scraps relating to
Philadelphia history, including newspaper clippings, illustrations, and
photographs, all neatly indexed.

A not dissimilar collection came as the result of the foresight of the
librarian, Lloyd P. Smith. In 1885 he presented the library with 400
bound volumes of pamphlets, and after his death in 1886 his widow
sold about as many more volumes to the trustees of the Loganian
Library for $300. Covering the political, social, economic, and phil-

William and Frederick Langenheim, *Girard Bank*. Daguerreotype, Philadelphia, 1844. Gift of John A. McAllister, 1896. This view of militia gathering in the wake of an anti-Catholic riot is Philadelphia's first news photograph.

anthropic life of the country—but naturally richest in local publications—these illuminated many facets of the half-century 1830–1880.

In 1886, Mary Rebecca Darby Smith, another descendant of James Logan and a cousin of Lloyd P. Smith, bequeathed her library of over 600 volumes, consisting mainly of literature and history, to the Loganian collection. Most of the volumes were presentation copies from their authors. Her autograph collection of nineteenth-century celebrities was also part of the gift. Anne Hampton Brewster, nineteenth-century fiction writer and one of the first female foreign correspondents to American newspapers, made the Library Company the beneficiary of her will in 1892. Brewster, a member of the Library Company for forty-one years and a friend of Lloyd P. Smith, left her entire library of approximately 2,000 volumes, as well as manuscripts, journals, notebooks, newspaper clippings, and all of her apartment furnishings. Brewster's library consisted mainly of European histories, and

PROVISIONAL
CONSTITUTION
AND
ORDINANCES
FOR THE
PEOPLE OF THE UNITED STATES.

PREAMBLE.

Whereas, Slavery, throughout its entire existence in the United States, is none other than a most barbarous, unprovoked, and unjustifiable War of one portion of its citizens upon another portion; the only conditions of which are perpetual imprisonment, and hopeless servitude or absolute extermination; in utter disregard and violation of those eternal and self-evident truths set forth in our Declaration of Independence: Therefore,

WE, CITIZENS OF THE UNITED STATES, AND THE OPPRESSED PEOPLE, WHO, BY A RECENT DECISION OF THE SUPREME COURT ARE DECLARED TO HAVE NO RIGHTS WHICH THE WHITE MAN IS BOUND TO RESPECT; TOGETHER WITH ALL OTHER PEOPLE DEGRADED BY THE LAWS THEREOF, DO, FOR THE TIME BEING ORDAIN AND ESTABLISH FOR OURSELVES, THE FOLLOWING PROVISIONAL CONSTITUTION AND ORDINANCES, THE BETTER TO PROTECT OUR PERSONS, PROPERTY, LIVES, AND LIBERTIES; AND TO GOVERN OUR ACTIONS:

ARTICLE I.

QUALIFICATIONS FOR MEMBERSHIP.

ALL persons of mature age, whether Proscribed, oppressed and enslaved Citizens, or of the Proscribed
A

John Brown, *Provisional Constitution and Ordinances for the People of the United States.* [St. Catherines, Ontario: William Howard Day, 1858]. Gift of Lloyd P. Smith, 1883.

Mary Rebecca Darby Smith. Frontispiece from *Leaves from the Past.* Philadelphia: J. B. Lippincott & Co., 1872. Gift of the author.

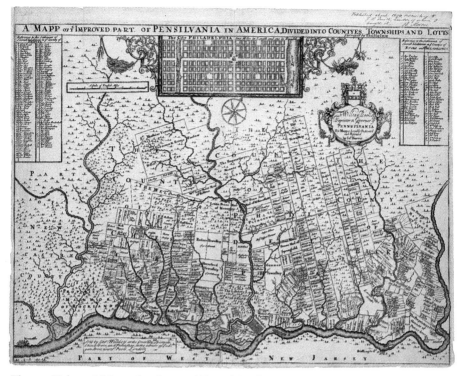

Thomas Holme, *A Mapp of ye Improved Part of Pensilvania in America.* Engraving,
London: Geo. Willdey, ca. 1700. Purchased ca. 1890.

Jans Adolf Jerichau, *Anne
Hampton Brewster.* Pencil on
paper, 1872. Brewster bequest,
1892.

her personal papers chronicle the life of an unmarried professional woman as well as the lives of the American expatriates in Rome on whom she reported for eighteen years.

Two bequests added specialized collections. Albert G. Emerick, a pioneer American musicologist, left his books to the Library Company in 1896, and in 1904 the library received from Charles G. Sower, a descendant of the country's first German printer, a family collection that was rich in Pennsylvania-German imprints.

With two buildings to operate, Lloyd P. Smith had at first divided his time between the Locust Street and Christian Street libraries. George Maurice Abbot, who had been hired as a boy to help in the

James Smither, *Benjn. Randolph, Cabinet Maker.* Engraved trade card, Philadelphia, [1769].

Edward Williams Clay, *"The Times."* Lithograph, New York, 1837.

old Library Hall, was soon sent down to supervise the Ridgway Library.
J. Bunford Samuel was taken on as a stack boy and messenger there.
Smith's successors—James G. Barnwell from 1887 to 1907 and the pa-
tient Abbot from 1907 to 1929—emigrated as soon as they could to
the more socially rewarding milieu of Locust Street. Few of the directors and few of the members gave much thought to the dusty vastness
of the gray Greek temple in which James and Phoebe Ann Rush were
entombed and, it sometimes seemed, in which the books were entombed also. They were satisfied to have Samuel take over the curatorship of the Ridgway Library.

Bunford Samuel was neither a professional librarian nor a formally
educated scholar, but he loved the books in his care. While others de-
pended on catalogue entries to know what books were on the shelves
and where to find them, Samuel over the years built up a memory bank
that was more efficient than the scattered arrangement and the separate catalogues. He was more like the European librarians of his day
than his contemporaries of the American Library Association; he was
primarily a defender of the books in his care. The curiosity seeker did
not find Samuel very helpful; the serious scholar received his serious
attention. The survival almost intact of the old books in the Library

Louis L. Peck. Tinted Lithograph, Philadelphia, ca. 1855.

Company is due, in no small measure, to Samuel's concern for half a century.

On the other hand, the main concern of the directors and the head librarian was seeing that the members were supplied with the most recent books for their leisure-time reading. After the Free Library of Philadelphia opened its main building on Chestnut Street in 1895 and later moved to 13th and Locust Streets, the Library Company was destined to drift. Its members became resigned to seeing it as an institution of undistinguished gentility. It was recorded in 1895 that fewer people had used the library and fewer books were taken out than usual. "The library facilities of the city have become so much enlarged during the past few years," the directors reported to the shareholders in 1903, "that a library of the character of your institution cannot hold the same position that it formerly did, when libraries were fewer in number." As an afterthought they added that, however, as "a library for the student and the thoughtful reader" its position remained preeminent. This statement summarized the library's history for the first part of the twentieth century. In his brief history of the Library Company published in 1913, Abbot noted that the number of books in its collections was 237,677, divided equally between the two buildings, and that there were 909 members and "many subscribers." Regular purchases, chiefly of popular works of fiction and nonfiction, buttressed by a considerable number of solid biographies and monographs on American history, continued to increase the library's holdings.

In 1929, Austin K. Gray became librarian. A gentle, cultured Englishman and literary historian, he attempted to rouse the library from its lethargy with lectures and exhibitions. However, he was unable to prevent the Library Company from inching toward bankruptcy

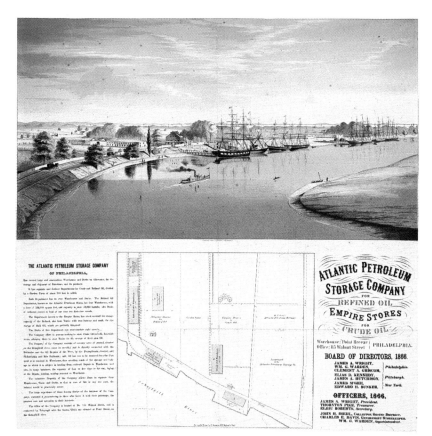

Atlantic Petroleum Storage Company. Chromolithograph, Philadelphia, [1866].

[The Homilies of Michael].
Ethiopian manuscript,
Gondar, ca. 1682. Gift
of Countess Van
Cuelenbroeck, 1900.

Austin K. Gray. Passport photograph,
1930. Librarian from 1931 to 1943.

as the Great Depression deepened. The real estate holdings of the Rush Estate, mostly in a deteriorating section of the city, melted away. Income from dues ($8 a year) and from a small endowment failed by a wide margin to meet expenditures; capital was invaded to pay bills. The publication of a history of the Library Company, written and considerably romanticized by Gray, sparked a gallant fund-raising effort and membership campaign, which managed to keep the institution afloat until the situation became too desperate for palliative measures—this despite the efforts of the Women's Committee, which was credited in the *Annual Report* for 1934 with extending the membership and activities of the Library Company.

In 1935, under the leadership of Owen Wister, then president of the Library Company, the directors urged that the Juniper and Locust Street building be given up and all the books concentrated in the Ridgway Library. They recommended "a policy whereby the Library, from being a general circulating library of current and ephemeral books, becomes a Library dedicated to the care of and making additions to its remarkable collections of valuable books." Even if such a policy did not please the majority of the shareholders, it was inevitable that it would prevail. Under the will of Arthur K. Lea in 1938 the Company received $50,000 "as a means towards a more aggressive administration of its library, so that said library may occupy a more conspicuous part in the educational facilities of the city and perform a more useful service than it has done in the past."

A further thrust in the direction of change was given by a grant from the Carnegie Corporation to recatalogue and reshelve the library so that its scholarly resources would be more readily available. Unfortunately, the program carried out with WPA (Works Progress Administration) help was not well conceived or executed. The old printed catalogues, the paper slips of the nineteenth century, and current cards were consolidated into a single author card catalogue. However, the entries were simply copied from the original entries. None was checked against a book on the shelf, and the whole was never edited to provide uniformity or to correct errors. Furthermore, the shelf location was not placed on the main card but had to be found by reference to a second catalogue arranged by serial numbers only. These cards went to the National Union Catalogue in Washington, D.C., and are the only record there, inaccurate and incomplete as they are, of the Library Company's holdings. At the time, no one looked upon the results of the Carnegie grant as anything but strengthening the status and stature of the Ridgway Library and its research materials.

At the annual meeting on May 1, 1939, the members unanimously agreed that the directors be given authority to sell or lease the Locust Street property. A small circulating library was to be retained in the center of the city for the members' convenience. During the following year, all the books were moved to the basement of the Ridgway Library under the supervision of Barney Chesnick. He had been hired to assist Samuel at Broad and Christian Streets and succeeded him in charge of the old collections, which were then being used by a comparatively few discerning and imaginative scholars. Chesnick was Samuel's spiritual successor as well; he matched his preceptor in concern for the books in his care and in his computer-like knowledge of their whereabouts. The labyrinthine arrangement of the shelves was made even more confusing by the expedients used to house the books from the uptown library. That building, empty, was torn down; the land was leased as a parking lot. The two-centuries-old Library Company was at the nadir of its fortunes.

About this time, two studies—one by Robert H. Downs, then librarian of New York University, and the other by the Bibliographical Planning Committee of Philadelphia under Charles W. David—looked at the Library Company's holdings and operations. They came to similar conclusions: that the circulation of modern books to members and subscribers was an obsolete service and that the Library Company should become a research library, preferably in association with one of the city's other institutions.

This required long-term planning. For the moment, the rent from the parking lot and income from endowment funds were not sufficient to pay for all the library's operating expenses. This situation, World War II, and Austin Gray's resignation as Librarian impelled the directors in 1943 to make an arrangement with the Free Library of Philadelphia whereby it became the corporate librarian of the Library Company, responsible (for a fee) for the administration of the library. The Free Library also opened a branch in the Ridgway Library. With Barney Chesnick in the service, the scholarly aspects of the Library Company were entrusted to the young historian John H. Powell, who

John Dickinson's

7 august 1787

WE the People of the States of New-Hampſhire, Maſſachuſetts, Rhode-Iſland and Providence Plan-tations, Connecticut, New-York, New-Jerſey, Penn-ſylvania, Delaware, Maryland, Virginia, North-Caro-lina, South-Carolina, and Georgia, do ordain, declare and eſtabliſh the following Conſtitution for the Govern-ment of Ourſelves and our Poſterity.

A R T I C L E   I.

The ſtile of this Government ſhall be, " The United States of America."

II.

The Government ſhall conſiſt of ſupreme legiſlative, executive and judicial powers.

III.

The legiſlative power ſhall be veſted in a Congreſs, to conſiſt of two ſeparate and diſtinct bodies of men, a Houſe of Repreſentatives, and a Senate ; each of which ſhall, in all caſes, have a negative on the other. The Legiſlature ſhall meet on the firſt Monday in December in every year, *unleſs a different day ſhall be appointed by law.*

IV.

Sect. 1. The Members of the Houſe of Repreſentatives ſhall be choſen eve-ry ſecond year, by the people of the ſeveral States comprehended within this Union. The qualifications of the electors ſhall be the ſame, from time to time, as thoſe of the electors in the ſeveral States, of the moſt numerous branch of their own legiſlatures.

Sect. 2. Every Member of the Houſe of Repreſentatives ſhall be of the age of twenty-five years at leaſt all have been a citizen in the United States for at leaſt three years before his election; and ſhall be, at the time of his e-lection, a reſident of the State in which he ſhall be choſen.

Sect. 3. The Houſe of Repreſentatives ſhall, at its firſt formation, and until the number of citizens and inhabitants ſhall be taken in the manner herein af-ter deſcribed, conſiſt of ſixty-five Members, of whom three ſhall be choſen in New-Hampſhire, eight in Maſſachuſetts, one in Rhode-Iſland and Providence Plantations, five in Connecticut, ſix in New-York, four in New-Jerſey, eight in Pennſylvania, one in Delaware, ſix in Maryland, ten in Virginia, five in North-Carolina, five in South-Carolina, and three in Georgia.

Sect. 4. As the proportions of numbers in the different States will alter from time to time; as ſome of the States may hereafter be divided; as others may be enlarged by addition of territory ; as two or more States may be united; as new States will be erected within the limits of the United States, the Legiſla-ture ſhall, in each of theſe caſes, regulate the number of repreſentatives by the number of inhabitants, according to the proviſions herein after made, at the rate of one for every forty thouſand, *provided that each State hath one Repreſentative.*

Sect. 5. All bills for raiſing or appropriating money, and for fixing the ſala-ries of the officers of government, ſhall originate in the Houſe of Repreſenta-tives, and ſhall not be altered or amended by the Senate. No money ſhall be drawn from the public Treaſury, but in purſuance of appropriations that ſhall originate in the Houſe of Repreſentatives.

Sect. 6. The Houſe of Repreſentatives ſhall have the ſole power of impeach-ment. It ſhall chooſe its Speaker and other officers.

Sect. 7. Vacancies in the Houſe of Repreſentatives ſhall be ſupplied by writs of election from the executive authority of the State, in the repreſentation from which they ſhall happen.   V.

U. S. *Constitution.* First printed draft. Philadelphia, August 7, 1787. John Dickinson's copy with his manuscript notes. Gift of Robert R. Logan, 1943.

at the same time was a research assistant with the Free Library. He wrote several monographs on the collections, including a survey of the large archive of the diplomat John Meredith Read, and he compiled a calendar of the papers of John Dickinson, which the Library Company received as a gift from Robert R. Logan. The latter, with the drafts of such significant state documents as the Continental Congress's first and second addresses to the King and Dickinson's annotated copies of the printed preliminary drafts of the Constitution, is a treasure house of prime historical importance. At about the same time the Library Company's endowment funds were reorganized and brilliantly reinvested by Moncure Biddle, who in concert with the treasurer, W. Logan Fox, began to build a solid financial base for the institution.

The resurgent feeling that "something should be done" had been repressed during the 1930s and 1940s because the Library Company's financial difficulties precluded any constructive change. During the war, some of the Library Company's most valuable treasures had been placed in the custody of the Free Library, and informal thought was given to the possibility that the Library Company might become the Free Library's rare book collection. However, in 1952, aided by an increasing flow of income from the parking garage that had been erected on the Locust Street property, the directors found themselves in a position to plan for the future and do something about it. They sought the advice and guidance of a number of experts. First, Edwin Wolf 2nd, formerly with the rare book firm of Rosenbach, was engaged to make a survey of the collections, to assess their scope, size, and importance, and to suggest means to improve their care and usefulness. Then, four eminent librarians—Lloyd A. Brown of the Peabody Institute, William A. Jackson of Harvard, Paul North Rice of the New York Public Library, and Clifford K. Shipton of the American Antiquarian Society—were invited to inspect the Library Company and consult with the directors about its future.

Unanimously, the experts agreed that the Library Company's greatest strength lay in its rare books and manuscripts and that its greatest contribution to society would be as a scholarly research library with special emphasis on American history and culture. There was no doubt that the rare books and manuscripts were far more numerous and more valuable than had been generally believed. The first and immediate

Edwin Wolf 2nd. Photograph, 1952. Librarian from 1955 to 1984.

step the consultants urged was a program of rehabilitation. The most valuable books should be taken from the scattered locations, recatalogued, repaired, and temporarily reshelved in a room to be refitted and air-conditioned. Then the experts recommended that the Library Company reduce and refine its mass of late-nineteenth- and twentieth-century books, keeping only those that would supplement as reference works the basic historical collections.

These steps were considered preliminary to a decision to move out of the Ridgway Library. That structure, once considered fireproof, was now judged to be a firetrap. Furthermore, the roof leaked, the basement was damp, and the building's location in the city was unfortunate. The consensus was that the Library Company should move to modern quarters in or adjacent to another compatible library as soon as possible. Meanwhile, it was recommended that the best be made of the physical facilities and work begun on rehabilitating the books and replacing the inadequate WPA catalogue. In January 1953, Wolf was appointed curator to carry out the program of revitalization.

As the shelves began to be searched, the richness of the collection became apparent to a greater degree. While it was known in bibliographical circles that the Library Company possessed American, and particularly Philadelphia and Pennsylvania, rarities, the quantity and quality of these had never been adequately judged. It had not been known how extensive were the holdings in the mathematical sciences, botany, medicine, and architecture and the useful arts; how many of the volumes had provenances of distinction—scores of books came from the libraries of Benjamin Franklin, William Byrd of Westover, Isaac Norris II, John Dickinson, and Benjamin Rush and, surprisingly, others had belonged to Ben Jonson, George Sandys, and Henry Vaughan; what unexpected, isolated treasures of English literature and history there were; and what a potential source of funds lay in the hun-

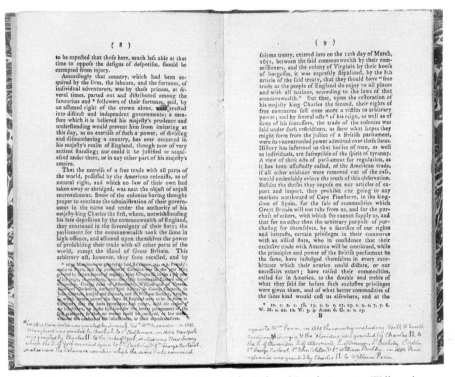

[Thomas Jefferson], *A Summary View of the Rights of British America*. Williamsburg: Printed by Clementina Rind, [1774]. With Jefferson's manuscript corrections, acquired before 1789.

William Shakespeare, *Plays and Poems*. Philadelphia, 1795–96. Thomas McKean's copy, with stencilled American eagles, signed at the foot of the spines by the binder, John Lightbody of Philadelphia. Purchased 1954.

dreds of duplicates. In these years, during which all pre-1700 books and eighteenth-century American imprints were scrutinized and re-catalogued on a priority basis, hardly a day went by when some exciting find did not surface: two copies of Thomas Jefferson's first published work with his manuscript corrections; books printed by the early Parisian printer Antoine Vérard; a history of Louisiana that Lewis and Clark took with them across the continent; and almost all Isaac Newton's writings in their first printings.

By 1955, with income from the parking garage increasing, the Library Company could stand on its own feet. In December of that year the arrangement with the Free Library was amicably terminated. Wolf became Librarian. As he wrote in his first *Annual Report*, for the year 1955, the old library was a phoenix reborn. He shared the excitement of rediscovery and revitalization with an audience of bibliophiles—librarians, collectors, booksellers, and, of course, members of the Library Company—through his paradoxically light yet scholarly essays in the *Annual Reports*. When duplicates were first identified as such and sold, the directors agreed that all moneys received from book sales would be used solely for the purchase of rare books to strengthen the permanent research collections and for binding pamphlets. Wolf blended the announcement of significant acquisitions by purchase and by gift with news of the Library Company's latest finds on its own shelves. One of the most significant of the latter-day acquisitions was a large portion of the Americana collection of W. Logan Fox, which came as a gift in 1962–1964. Over the years the *Annual Reports* of the Library Company have been widely circulated at home and abroad, and they remain the chief medium through which the institution makes itself and its books known.

The experts' primary recommendation—to move from the totally inadequate and unsuitable Ridgway Library—had not been forgotten.

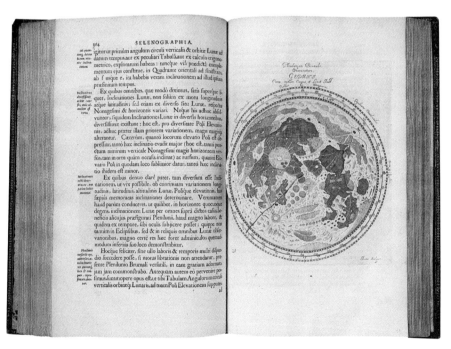

Johannes Hevelius, *Selenographia*. Danzig, 1647. With movable volvelles. Purchased 1955.

Taufschein for Elisabeth Romich. [Frederick, Md.: Matthias Bärtgis, 1786]. George Allen Collection, purchased 1959.

Conversations took place and preliminary studies were made of the practicability and advantages of locating in the vicinity of the University of Pennsylvania, the American Philosophical Society (which had just recreated for its own use the Library Company's eighteenth-century building on Fifth Street), or the Historical Society of Pennsylvania. Eminent rare book librarians and historians were again consulted for advice. Ten of eleven favored a location next to the Historical Society; only one preferred another site. Consequently, at the annual meeting of the Library Company on May 2, 1960, urged to do so by the president, Nicholas B. Wainwright, and the directors, the members voted overwhelmingly to authorize the directors to petition the Orphan's Court for permission to sell the Ridgway Library and to erect a new library on Locust Street adjacent to the Historical Society.

The steps necessary to bring the plan to fruition were interlocking and complicated. Fortunately, at the critical time the City of

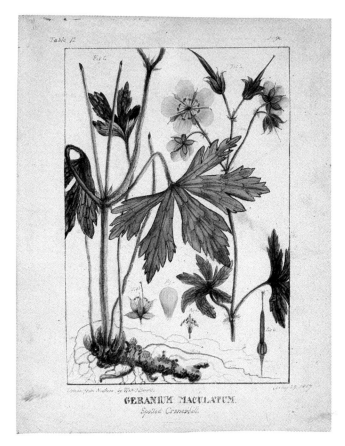

Table 1.

Fig. 1.   Fig. 2.

GERANIUM MACULATUM.
Spotted Cranesbill.

William P. C. Barton,
*"Geranium
Maculatum"* for
*Vegetable Materia
Medica.* Watercolor,
ca. 1817. Gift of
Elizabeth S. Abbot, 1961.

Philadelphia made a satisfactory offer for the building and land. An elaborate, lengthy legal brief, justifying the sale and the move, was presented to the Orphan's Court, which according to the Rush will had to approve all sales of real estate. After a full-dress hearing, the Library Company was given permission to make the sale and also to use such other funds as were part of the Rush estate to build the new library. Three nineteenth-century brownstone houses, owned by and contiguous to the Historical Society, were purchased and torn down. Plans for a modern eight-story building were drawn by the architectural firm of Carroll, Grisdale, and Van Alen, and construction began in 1964. Meanwhile, to carry out another of the original recommendations concerning the future of the Library Company and to avoid moving unwanted books, a sweep of the shelves was undertaken. With formal authorization from the directors and the membership as a whole, Wolf culled and disposed of works printed after 1880 that were deemed not germane to the Library Company's main collections. Perhaps as many as 100,000 volumes were removed and sold, the largest segment by far consisting of novels. One of the most unusual events in the process of relocation was the transfer of the remains of James and Phoebe Ann Rush from a crypt at the Ridgway Library to a crypt beneath the Locust Street building.

With the holdings whittled down to an estimated 375,000 volumes, the Library Company was ready to return to the center of the city. The new building was completed by the end of 1965. The transfer of the books, though difficult, provided an opportunity to revamp the shelving arrangement and gather together subject classes that the space problems in the old building had fragmented. Because approximately two-thirds of the funds for the new library derived from the Rush estate, the building, like its predecessor, was named the Ridgway Library. The building was opened to the public in April 1966. A reciprocal arrangement was reached with the neighboring Historical Society whereby its rare books are shelved and used by readers in the Library Company, and the latter's manuscripts are shelved and used by readers in the Historical Society.

With the transfer of the collections to the new Ridgway Library, the goals set in 1952 by Wolf and the other consultants had been achieved. In an amazingly short time, the venerable circulating library had been utterly transformed into a research library specializing in American history and culture and its European background up to roughly the Civil War. Before 1860 this had been the largest public library in America, and the collections were already strong in all areas. It had become apparent, however, that the Library Company's decline in the 1860s and 1870s had resulted in a much spottier collection. The post-1880 materials had largely been deaccessioned. The exchange of books and manuscripts with the Historical Society committed the Library Company to remaining primarily a collection of printed materials. Thus the library's mission was defined.

This mission implied a blueprint for future growth based on the principle of building to strength. The opening of the new building in 1966 was marked by an exhibition called *Bibliothesauri: Or, Jewels from the Shelves of the Library Company of Philadelphia;* included were new acquisitions as well as rarities discovered in the course of recataloguing and rearranging the collections for research. The new acquisitions resonated with the core collection in ways that articulated its complex and distinctive character. Wolf's conception of the collection, and hence the types of books he added to it, had been evolving for a decade and was to change considerably in the decade to come.

From his first visit as a consultant, Wolf focused on the older collections and on the era of the library's foundation. Here was the only major colonial library to survive nearly intact; what could it reveal about the intellectual world of the eighteenth century? From 1954 to 1956, Wolf published several articles about the selection of books in the early years of the Library Company, as well as a facsimile of the 1741 catalogue printed by Franklin. His first new acquisitions were replacements for books that had been listed in the early catalogues but were no longer on the shelves. Many a book that had cost five shillings in the 1750s was bought for the same price two centuries later in the depressed postwar London book market. To round out this ideal enlightenment library, Wolf also bought first editions of important works of early science and erudition of which the Library Company had only later editions or none at all.

This same interest in eighteenth-century intellectual history led Wolf in 1956 to begin the reconstruction of three colonial private libraries that had been partly or wholly incorporated into the Library Company: those of James Logan, Benjamin Franklin, and William Byrd of Westover, Virginia. Wolf published a definitive catalogue of Logan's library in 1974. The other two libraries had been scattered by 1800, but he was able to locate substantial parts of them on the Library Company's shelves and in other collections across the country. (An exhibition of books owned by Franklin, based on Wolf's still unpublished card file, was mounted in 1990 as *Poor Richard's Books*.)

The study of provenance gave new meaning to the Library Company's collections. Books that had been owned by a host of other colonial and early national figures were located on the shelves or were received as gifts over the years. In 1959, Wolf published a catalogue of the Library Company's holdings of books that were in (or omitted from) Wing's *Short Title Catalogue* of British books, 1641–1700; he indexed the provenance of all 4,000 titles, thus uncovering complex patterns in the movement of seventeenth-century British books through eighteenth-century American private libraries. The only public col-

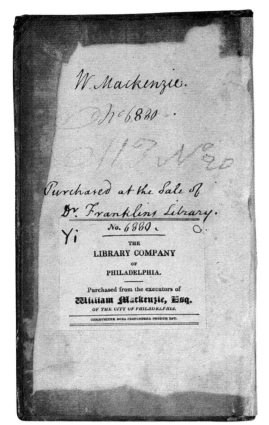

William Smith, *Discourses on Several Public Occasions*. London, 1759. Mackenzie bequest, 1828. The pencilled shelfmark, C113 N20, on the pastedown endpaper was the key to Edwin Wolf's reconstruction of Franklin's library.

lection of books in the city before the Library Company's founding was the parish library at Christ Church, which included some 800 books given in 1700 by the English philanthropist Thomas Bray. It still survived, and shortly after the move to Locust Street it was placed on deposit in the Library Company. Meanwhile, Wolf began privately to accumulate data about who owned what books in colonial Philadelphia and to assemble a collection (which he donated in 1989) of the books that were most commonly owned. All this data was methodically presented in Wolf's 1985 Lyell Lectures in Bibliography at Oxford University, published as *The Book Culture of a Colonial American City*.

This vision of the Library Company as a microcosm of eighteenth-century American book culture embraced only the older part of the

Book from Christ Church Library, donated by the Rev. Thomas Bray ca. 1700, deposited with the Library Company 1966.

collection and did not account for the Library Company's later development. During the 1960s, recataloguing proceeded chronologically, and the wealth of the nineteenth-century collections emerged. For the first time the *Annual Reports* began to mention a few early nineteenth-century acquisitions. In the 1960 *Annual Report*, Wolf somewhat daringly predicted that some day a speech by Daniel Webster or a memorial by Dorothea Dix would be sought out by rare book libraries. In 1963 he published a catalogue of the thousands of song sheets from 1850–1870 in the McAllister scrapbooks. Soon he was buying nineteenth-century books in quantity.

The widening scope of acquisitions went hand in hand with new ways of seeing the collections and presenting them to the world. In 1969, Wolf mounted an exhibition called *Negro History: 1553–1903*.

The preface to the catalogue began with a manifesto: "Everybody is *talking* about Negro history, so we decided to *do* something about it." The exhibition was so successful that the entire collection was combed in the following three years, with the help of a Ford Foundation Grant, and everything relating to African American history was catalogued: early European accounts of Africa and the Atlantic slave trade, the economy of slavery, antislavery and abolition literature, apologias for slavery, the antebellum politics of slavery, slave narratives, documents of urban free black communities (especially that in Philadelphia, the largest), materials relating to Reconstruction and the "Negro question," and literature by and about black Americans. Most of this ma-

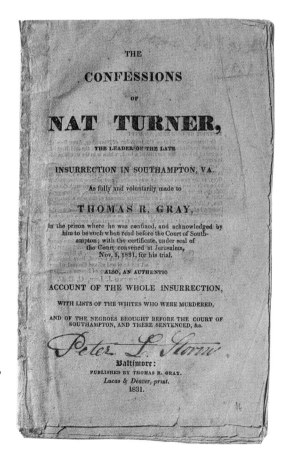

Nat Turner, *Confessions*. Baltimore, 1831. Purchased 1974.

terial had been classified in other ways: travels, politics, autobiography, etc. By seeing this material in a new way, by recovering the common thread that linked these diverse books, a subject collection of surprising strength was formed. *Afro-Americana, 1553–1906*, with 16,500 entries, appeared over the imprint of G. K. Hall in 1973. It immediately became a standard bibliography of the subject and has remained so, even though it has been out of print for many years. Since then, another 2,000 books and other materials have been added to the collection. It has attracted more scholars from greater distances than any other collection in the Library Company.

In the following years, other "special collections" were uncovered in the general collection. In the late 1970s, with a grant from the Andrew W. Mellon Foundation, the collections were again searched, and catalogues were published in four areas: American education, philanthropy, agriculture, and natural history, all before 1860. These were all areas in which existing bibliography was weak, scholarly interest was intense, market prices were low, and the Library Company's collecting had historically been outstandingly strong. The catalogues included the collections of the Historical Society and the American Philosophical Society, thus sowing the seeds of future interlibrary cooperation and making it easy to acquire more books in those areas without unnecessary duplication. As with the Afro-Americana collection, these catalogues reunited bodies of literature that crossed several disciplinary boundaries. For example, the education and philanthropy catalogues are in effect bibliographies of voluntary organizations, even of a broad movement of social reform that permeated every aspect of antebellum society.

Comparing the Library Company's holdings with already-published subject bibliographies uncovered still more collections of surprising strength in areas such as technology, Judaica, household and cookery books, courtesy books, gift books, architecture, women's history, and German-Americana. The 1974 exhibition *Women, 1500 to 1900* was as pioneering in its way as *Negro History*. The exhibition explored such themes as women as emblems of good and evil, images of women in advertising and iconography, women's reading habits, prostitution, fashion and grooming, religion, education, sports, marriage and divorce, domestic life, single women, literary women, women in the arts and social reform, the struggle for equal rights and the suffrage, and women in the work force. In 1983 the Library Company became head-quarters for Werner Tannhof's compilation of a bibliography of German-American imprints through 1830. The Sower Collection, mentioned above, had been supplemented by huge collections of German-Americana purchased from George Allen in 1959 and Wilbur Oda in 1961. Together with the collection of the Historical Society on deposit with the Library Company, this turned out to be by far the largest collection of German-Americana when the first two volumes of the bibliography were published by the Göttingen University Library in 1989 as *The First Century of German Language Printing in the United States of America.*

Hoch-Deutsches Lutherishes ABC. Germantown, 1802. George Allen Collection, purchased 1959.

In the process of strengthening and extending the Library Company's core collection, unnecessary or expensive duplication of other libraries' holdings was always avoided. This principle was applied not only to individual books but to whole areas of collecting. For example, the Library Company's core collection of American medicine is superb up to about 1820, but thereafter it yielded responsibility for collecting in that area to the College of Physicians. The bequest of Benjamin Rush's library by his son James further enriched the pre-1820 collection. Austin's bibliography of American medical imprints up to 1820, published in 1961, revealed the Library Company's strength. Today, no attempt is made to collect medicine after 1820, but the earlier collection has been developed vigorously, to the point at which it is difficult to find anything to buy. In the same way, children's books and Western Americana are left to the Free Library and manuscripts to the Historical Society. The vast field of American literature is easily shared with the University of Pennsylvania without expensive duplication; the Library Company's collection is smaller but is currently growing faster, in response to scholarly interest in popular and non-canonical writing.

Marie Korey, who came to work as curator of printed books in 1972, played a major role in analyzing the Library Company's strengths and choosing new subject areas to open up for development. She left in 1983 to become head of the rare book department at the Free Library of Philadelphia. Her successor, James Green, has continued to build the collections in the main areas marked out by Wolf and Korey, as well as in other areas that were not previously cultivated so intensively, such as economics, philosophy, popular fiction, popular medicine, photographic literature (in support of the Print Department), books by women, and illustrated books. All acquisitions still build on the core collection acquired between 1731 and 1880, as described incidentally throughout this volume. The collection is constantly growing and adapting to new currents in scholarship, but its essential character has not changed. In the past forty years, over 30,000 books have been added to the rare book collection, including gifts as well as purchases, and as many more to the reference collection. The total holdings approach half a million volumes.

The Library Company's increased visibility has attracted gifts of major significance. In 1976, Jean Hoopes Epstein presented the European

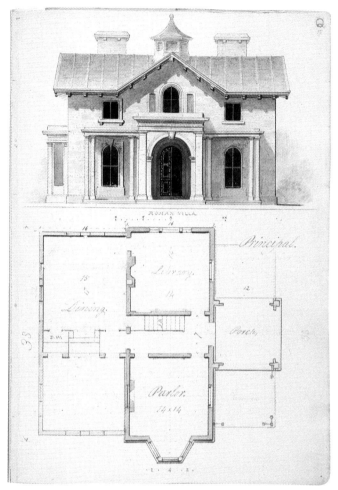

Alexander Jackson Davis, *Rural Residences*. New York, 1837. Gift of Anthony N. B. Garvan, 1978. Unique copy, with extra ink-and-wash plans.

books of science and technology collected by her father, Penrose R. Hoopes. The next major gift came in 1980, when Librarian Wolf presented his extensive collection of early American Judaica, consisting of manuscripts, books, and broadsides printed in America from 1718 to 1875. In 1982 the Chew family formally turned over to the Library Company the books at Cliveden, their handsome Georgian mansion in the Germantown section of Philadelphia. The volumes include the law library of Benjamin Chew, colonial chief justice of Pennsylvania, as well as books and vast quantities of pamphlets owned by his son

THAUMALEA OBSCURA

Daniel Giraud Elliot,
Phasianidae. New York,
1872. Gift of Mrs.
Wharton Sinkler,
1976.

Benjamin, his grandson, William White Chew, and William Tilghman, a relative by marriage and later chief justice.

More recently, the Library Company received the spectacular collections of ornithological plate books of Louise Elkins Sinkler and Francis R. Cope, Jr. Mrs. H. Lea Hudson contributed numerous pamphlets and books written or published by Mathew Carey, as well as a portrait of Carey by John Neagle. And Mrs. Robert R. Price, Jr., a descendant of the Rittenhouse family that established the first paper mill in America along the banks of Wissahickon Creek near Germantown in 1690, presented to the Library Company the archive documenting that early industry.

Important collections have also arrived as long-term deposits by institutions that recognize the Library Company's ability to provide care

John Gould, *Birds of Great Britain*. London, 1873. Collection of Francis R. Cope, Jr., 1992.

Joseph Ben Gurion, *History of the Jews*. Boston, [1722]. Gift of Edwin Wolf 2nd, 1980.

for such collections. Among those deposits are the historical libraries of Christ Church, St. Peter's Church, Girard College, and the Wagner Free Institute of Science.

The move to the spacious, pleasant quarters of the new Ridgway Library proved fruitful for the Library Company's print collection as well. With the appointment of Stefanie A. Munsing as curator of prints in 1971, the Print Department was born and quickly became a center of activity. The new curator faced the vast task of reorganizing and cataloguing the accumulation of Philadelphia views, portraits, American political cartoons, and early photographs. When Munsing moved on to the print collections of the Library of Congress in 1975, Bernard Reilly moved from the Reading Room to the Print

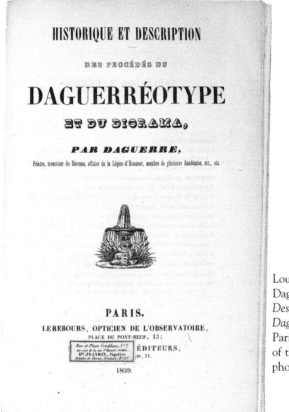

Louis Jacques Mandé Daguerre, *Historique et Description des Procédés du Daguerréotype et du Diorama.* Paris, 1839. First printing of the first description of photography.

Thomas Eakins, *Motion Studies*. Photograph, 1884. Gift of Elizabeth G. Coates, 1982.

Department. It was during his tenure and due to his initiative that the Library Company's remarkable collection of nineteenth-century Philadelphia photographs began to be appreciated.

In 1977, when the Library of Congress lured Reilly away, Kenneth Finkel took over the Print Department. Under his aggressive and imaginative curatorship from 1977 to 1994 the collection increased at a phenomenal rate. With the exhibition and simultaneous publication in 1980 of *Nineteenth-Century Photography in Philadelphia*, the Print Department became the center for the study of early photography in Philadelphia. A large archive of photographic negatives and manuscript notebooks of pioneer aerial photographer William Nicholson Jennings was brought together in the Library Company in two separate purchases in 1978 and 1981. In 1982, Miss Elizabeth G. Coates generously donated seven motion studies by Thomas Eakins. A substantial portion of the work of painter-photographer George Bacon

Wenderoth, Taylor & Brown, *Gallery of Arts & Manufactures*. Philadelphia, [1871]. Gift of S. Marguerite Brenner, 1984.

Wood, a contemporary of Eakins, came as the gift of his granddaughter, Elsie Wood Harmon, the same year. Through the generosity of Wawa, Inc. and its president, Richard D. Wood, Jr., twenty-eight daguerreotype portraits by some of the city's leading photographers were acquired. The Library Company had much to celebrate in the 1983 exhibition and catalogue, *Philadelphia ReVisions*. As a direct result of *ReVisions*, Virgil Kauffman gave a collection of almost 4,000 glass negatives, representing pictures taken in the Philadelphia area by his Aero Service Corporation.

Conservation of the ever-growing collections grew in importance over the years. A bindery was first set up at the Library Company in 1954 by the German master bookbinder Fritz Eberhardt to repair and

Robert Cornelius,
Grandma Toppan.
Daguerreotype,
ca. 1841.
Purchased 1986.

rebind in chronological order the vast collection of pamphlet Americana. After Eberhardt left in 1957 to work on his own, Kaspar Reder was hired to continue the work. The care of the print collection was taken up in 1971; the bindery staff worked under the guidance of Curator of Prints Stefanie Munsing, who had some training in conservation from Winterthur. Under Chief of Conservation Jennifer Woods Rosner, who came to the Library Company in 1980, the staff has begun to move systematically through the entire rare book collection, and its range of treatments has widened to include making protective boxes, reattaching covers detached from leather bindings, repairing cloth bindings of the 19th century, and replacing old library bindings with new ones made of high-quality archival materials.

The exhibition program became more formalized with the move to Locust Street. Jointly with the Historical Society and the American Philosophical Society an exhibition was held during the Bicentennial year, *A Rising People: The Founding of the United States, 1765–1789*, which drew upon the resources of the three historic institutions. In

Examples of the Craftsmanship of the Conservation Workshop. Photograph, 1995.

1983, *Germantown and the Germans*, a major exhibition and catalogue produced jointly by the Historical Society and the Library Company, celebrated the 300th anniversary of the founding of Germantown and the beginning of German settlement in America.

The climax of the new emphasis on exhibitions and public programs was the "Quarter of a Millennium" celebration in 1981. A symposium on "The Intellectual World of 1731" brought speakers not only from across the United States but also from the People's Republic of China, West Germany, Italy, and England to bring to life the era in which the Library Company was born. Representatives from some thirty national and university libraries throughout the world that had been founded before 1731 attended the events as the guests of the Library Company, while a host of members and friends participated in the reception, lectures, lunches, and banquet dinner that made up the celebration. A superb exhibition and its magnificently produced catalogue displayed 255 books, manuscripts, maps, prints, drawings, paintings, and furniture selected from the Library Company's 250-year accumulation of riches.

Under the direction of Librarian Wolf the Library Company assumed a leading role in the cultural and intellectual community of Philadelphia and established a reputation of scholarly service both locally and internationally. Wolf often referred to himself as *Dinosaurus Bibliothecarius*, a librarian of an antediluvian genus that is now all but extinct. There were profound changes in the way libraries were run in the 1960s and 1970s, and the Library Company was independent enough to be able to pick and choose which trends to follow and which to ignore. Franklinian common sense, with a dash of thrift, was its guide, as befitted a library struggling to be reborn. It remained, to use another Wolf metaphor, a "mom-and-pop library with a supermarket stock."

Wolf retired at the end of 1984 and was succeeded by John C. Van Horne, who came to the Library Company from the American Philosophical Society, where he was an editor of *The Papers of Benjamin*

John C. Van Horne.
Photograph, 1995.
Librarian from 1985.

Henry Latrobe. Under Van Horne's guidance the Library Company struck out in several new directions. It became a member of the Research Libraries Group (RLG) and began the long and arduous task of recataloguing its rare book holdings into RLG's computerized bibliographical database, known as RLIN. The Library Company also began to attract more scholars to the collections by instituting an endowed research fellowship program in 1987 that provides modest stipends to enable graduate students and senior scholars to travel to Philadelphia to work in the Library Company. The Library Company also created a revolving Publication Fund that supports the publication of a variety of works, usually carrying the joint imprint of the Library Company and a commercial or university press co-publisher.

The Rev. William Smith, *Valentine Poem to Elizabeth Graeme Ferguson,* 1759, transcribed in Ferguson's *Poemata Juvenilia.* Gift of Mrs. Howard Aley, 1985.

These books are generally based on the collections or relate to special projects or programs. For example, Dover Publications, Inc. in 1988 published a book in conjunction with the exhibition *Philadelphia: Then and Now*, which paired historic photographs with modern views taken from the same vantage points; and Cornell University Press published in 1994 *The Abolitionist Sisterhood: Women's Political Culture in Antebellum America*, a collection of essays that grew out of a symposium on the Anti-Slavery Conventions of American Women of 1837–1839.

Heeding Franklin's admonition to "join, or die," the Library Company has over the years confederated with many other institutions for various purposes. In 1972 the Library Company was one of the founding members of the Independent Research Libraries Association (IRLA). Now a consortium of more than a dozen member institutions—such as the Huntington, Folger, Morgan, and Newberry Libraries and the American Antiquarian Society—IRLA brings its directors together each year to discuss the common problems and needs of independent, privately supported research libraries, from fund raising and relationships with foundations and federal agencies to the conservation of library materials and the support of scholarship.

In 1985 the Library Company took a leading role in the formation of the Philadelphia Area Consortium of Special Collections Libraries (PACSCL). The first project of PACSCL was the ambitious 1988 exhibition *Legacies of Genius: A Celebration of Philadelphia Libraries*, which was displayed in the galleries of the Library Company and the Historical Society. This major exhibition featured treasures selected from the collections of the sixteen member institutions. PACSCL, at first an informal cooperative association, subsequently became a nonprofit corporation with twenty member institutions and is engaged in various collaborative undertakings.

In the early 1990s a major renovation of the nearly thirty-year-old building took place. The Print Department, which had been expanded in 1984 to keep pace with the rapid growth of the collection, was again doubled in size. The Lazzarini statue of Franklin was restored and once again became part of the façade in a new glass-fronted, street-level niche. The lobby and Reading Room were revamped to make them more inviting. A fire-suppression system and a new state-of-the-art security system were installed. Lastly, the nearly worn-out climate control system was largely replaced with equipment that will maintain

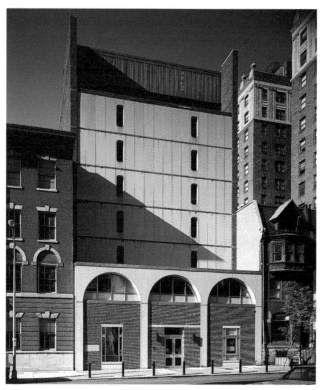

Façade of 1314 Locust Street Building. Photograph, 1995.

constant temperature and humidity throughout the building reliably and economically. These changes in the physical plant will ensure the preservation and continued usefulness of the collections.

In the second half of the twentieth century, the Library Company has been utterly transformed from a dusty mausoleum filled with books that were deteriorating from heat, damp, and dust, to a busy and vital center for research and education of national importance. Attractively arranged exhibitions interpret different aspects of the collections to the general public in provocative ways. Frequent public programs and scholarly publications reach large audiences. The Reading Room is a comfortable and dynamic environment in which to conduct research. The staff shares its extensive knowledge of the collections with visitors and learns from them in turn. The Library Company remains open and free of charge to any serious scholar, but the collections are now housed in closed stacks, and no rare materials circulate except as loans for exhibition in other institutions. The collections are constantly and vigorously expanded and enriched, and they are fully accessible through card catalogues and other in-house finding aids. Finally, the new computer catalogue holds out the promise of vastly superior access not only for those who visit the library in person, but also for scholars in their own offices and libraries throughout the world.

All these changes have been made in order to carry out the Library Company's new mission as articulated in the 1950s: to collect, preserve, and make available books, graphics, and other primary source materials for the study of American history and culture up to the closing years of the 19th century. Much has changed and will change, but one thing remains constant: the collections are the focus of all the library's energies, and the reason for its existence. Future generations of scholars will doubtless be as comfortable with computers as with books. Indeed, some speculate that the book as it has been known for more than half a millennium is on the road to extinction, soon to be replaced by the so-called "virtual library" and its promised electronic access to the cumulative wisdom of mankind. But surely in such a

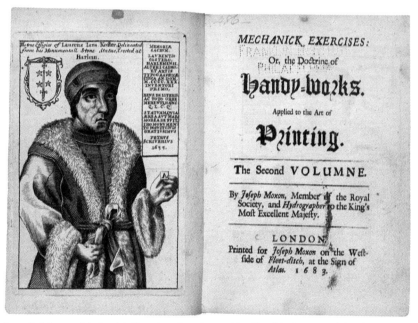

Joseph Moxon, *Mechanick Exercises*. London, 1683. Franklin's copy of the first printer's manual. Purchased 1986.

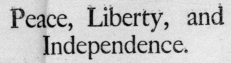

Peace, Liberty, and Independence.

PHILADELPHIA, MARCH 24, 1783.

Yesterday arrived, after a passage of 32 days from Cadiz, a French Sloop of War, commanded by M. Du Quesne, with the agreeable Intelligence of PEACE.

The particular Articles respecting this happy and glorious Event, are as follow:

The principal articles of the Preliminaries of the Peace, of the 20th of January, 1783.

FRANCE to retain Tobago and Senegal. France to restore to Great-Britain, Grenada, St. Vincents, Dominica, and St. Christophers.

St. Eustatia, Demarara, Barbice and Issequibo, to be restored to the Dutch.

Great-Britain to restore to France, Goree, St. Lucia, St. Pierre, and Miquelon.

The fishery of France and England on the coast of Newfoundland to remain on the same footing on which they were by the treaty of 1763, except that part of the coast, Cape Bonavista, at Cape St. John's, shall belong to the English.

France to be re-established in the East-Indies, as well in Bengal as on the east and west coast of the Peninsula, as regulated by the treaty of 1763.

The articles of the preceding treaties, concerning the demolition of Dunkirk, to be suppressed.

Spain to retain Minorca and West-Florida.

Great-Britain cedes East-Florida to Spain.

An agreement to be entered into between Spain and Great-Britain, about the cutting of wood in the Bay of Honduras.

Great-Britain to retain the Dutch settlement of Negapatnam, in the East-Indies.

Great-Britain to restore Trinquemale to the Dutch, if not re-taken.

St. Eustatia, Demarara, and Issequibo to be restored by the French to the United Provinces.

Great-Britain acknowledges the Sovereignty and Independence of the Thirteen United States of America.

The limits of the United States to be as agreed upon in the provisional articles between them and Great-Britain, except that they shall not extend farther down the river Mississippi than the 32d degree of north latitude, from whence a line is to be drawn to the head of the river St. Mary, and along the middle of that river down to its mouth.

Printed by E. OSWALD, at the Coffee-House.

Peace, Liberty, and Independence. Philadelphia, 1783. Only known copy of the first announcement of the preliminary peace agreement ending the Revolutionary War. Anonymous gift in memory of Elizabeth W. Bendiner, 1992.

world the book as object will gain in stature and intellectual value not only as the recognized source and vessel of that wisdom, but also as the essential source for its more ephemeral electronic cousins. In such a world institutions like the Library Company of Philadelphia that have been providing excellent stewardship of the nation's intellectual heritage and resources will continue to be indispensable.

LIBRARIANS

Louis Timothée (d. 1738)	November 14, 1732 – December 10, 1733
Benjamin Franklin (1706–1790)	December 10, 1733 – March 11, 1734
William Parsons (1701–1757)	March 11, 1734 – May 5, 1746
Robert Greenway	May 5, 1746 – June 13, 1763
John Edwards	July 11, 1763 – February 13, 1764
Francis Hopkinson (1737–1791)	February 13, 1764 – May 13, 1765
James Johnston	May 13, 1765 – May 9, 1768
Ludowick Sprogell	May 9, 1768 – November 13, 1769
John DeMauregnault	May 2, 1769 – August 5, 1771
William Attmore	August 5, 1771 – May 10, 1773
Charles Cist (1738–1805)	May 10, 1773 – March 7, 1774
Francis Daymon	April 14, 1774 – June 10, 1777
Samuel Lobdell	June 27, 1777 – December 8, 1778
John Todd, Sr.	December 8, 1778 – June 16, 1779
Bernard Fearis	June 24, 1779 – January 11, 1780
Joseph Fawcett	January 11, 1780 – January 13, 1784
John Todd, Jr. (1763–1793)	January 13, 1784 – February 3, 1785
Zachariah Poulson (1761–1844)	February 8, 1785 – March 6, 1806
George Campbell, Jr. (d. 1855)	April 10, 1806 – May 14, 1829
John Jay Smith (1798 – 1881)	May 14, 1829 – February 6, 1851
Lloyd Pearsall Smith (1822–1886)	February 6, 1851 – died July 2, 1886
James G. Barnwell	February 3, 1887 – November 7, 1907
George Maurice Abbot	November 7, 1907 – June 30, 1929
David C. Knoblauch	July 1, 1929 – October 1931 (acting librarian)
Austin K. Gray (1888–1945)	October 1, 1931 – March 31, 1943
Barney Chesnick (1909–1966)	April 1 – September 1943 (entered army)
Free Library of Philadelphia	November 16, 1943 – December 19, 1955
Edwin Wolf 2nd (1911–1991)	December 19, 1955 – December 31, 1984
John C. Van Horne (1950–)	January 1, 1985 –

A Note on the Text

This work is a revised and much expanded version of *At the Instance of Benjamin Franklin*, by Edwin Wolf 2nd, published by the Library Company with a grant from the William Penn Foundation in 1976. (A shorter version of Wolf's text had previously appeared in Volume XV of the *Encyclopedia of Library and Information Science*, New York, 1975. The Library Company is grateful to Marcel Dekker, Inc. for permission to reprint much of it here.) The new edition also includes passages from *The Wolf Years*, a continuation of the Library Company's history by Marie E. Korey, published in 1984 on the occasion of Wolf's retirement. The sections on the more recent history of the Library Company were written by John C. Van Horne and James Green, aided by other staff members. The photography is by Will Brown.

This edition was printed on Monadnock Paper Mills 70lb. Dulcet Smooth Text, an acid free paper, by the Printing Division of York Graphic Services, Inc. at 3600 West Market Street, York, Pennsylvania, 17404.

This book has been published with the assistance of the Library Company's Andrew W. Mellon Foundation Publication Fund.